ON SLEDGE AND
TO OUTCAST SIBE

Dedicating her journey to Queen Victoria, and armed with letters of recommendation from the Empress of Russia, Prince Ivan Golitsyn and the American Embassy in St Petersburg, Kate Marsden set out in 1890 to journey to Yakutsk, in north east Siberia, to give help to a colony of lepers, shunned by society.

As a member of a multi-national party, comprised of various religions and races, Kate Marsden describes how all differences were forgotten as they worked together to achieve their common objective. This is an extraordinary testament by a woman of great courage, and gives a fascinating insight into the world of pre-Revolutionary Russia.

Kate Marsden lived out her final years in England as an invalid and died in 1931.

Eric Newby is a celebrated traveller, and author of many books including *Slowly Down the Ganges*, *Time Off in Southern Italy*, *World Atlas of Exploration*, *The Big Red Train Ride*, *A Traveller's Life* and *On the Shores of the Mediterranean*.

To

HER MOST GRACIOUS AND IMPERIAL MAJESTY

THE QUEEN,

The most queenly woman and the most womanly Queen,
whose keen sympathy with suffering has made her,
personally, as beloved,
as the progress of the British Empire, under her rule,
has made her Throne magnificent,

THIS STORY

Of a woman's work
On behalf of helpless, hopeless, and homeless outcasts,
is,
With the most profound respect and humble gratitude,

DEDICATED.

ON SLEDGE AND HORSEBACK
TO OUTCAST SIBERIAN LEPERS

Kate Marsden

With an Introduction by Eric Newby

**PHOENIX
PRESS**

5 UPPER SAINT MARTIN'S LANE
LONDON
WC2H 9EA

A PHOENIX PRESS PAPERBACK

First published in Great Britain
by The Record Press in 1892
This paperback edition published in 2001
by Phoenix Press,
a division of The Orion Publishing Group Ltd,
Orion House, 5 Upper St Martin's Lane,
London WC2H 9EA

Introduction Copyright © 1986 by Eric Newby

A CIP catalogue record for this book
is available from the British Library.

Printed and bound in Great Britain by
Clays Ltd, St Ives plc

ISBN 1 84212 397 1

INTRODUCTION.

Kate Marsden's book, its title redolent of adventure, hardship and horror, is an account of an immense journey from Moscow to north-eastern Siberia and back undertaken in 1891 by a middle-aged nurse and missionary (she may have been older; her photographs don't tell us) to see for herself the conditions in which the lepers were living there and to try and improve their lot.

According to her own testimony—her book is singularly lacking in autobiographical detail—her first meeting with lepers was with some Bulgarians while she was at Constantinople during the Turco-Russian War, presumably that of 1876–77.

Her original intention in travelling to Yakutia in north-eastern Siberia was to seek out a herb which was reputed to grow there and was said to be a cure for leprosy. With its aid she hoped to alleviate the sufferings of the lepers of India, for which she was ultimately bound. She ended up trying to improve the lot of the lepers of Yakutia which, because of the extremes of heat and cold experienced there, was perhaps more miserable than that of lepers in some other parts of the world.

She arrived in Moscow in November 1890 wearing clothes suitable for an English winter, having travelled there by way of Jerusalem, Constantinople and the Caucasus, to find the temperature twenty degrees below zero.

Nevertheless, in spite of having the wrong clothes (she managed to borrow a *shouba*, a fur pelisse) she did have the right recommendations: from Queen Victoria, with whom she had an audience, and from Princess Alexandra of Wales who received her at Marlborough House and subsequently wrote a letter on her behalf to the then Empress of Russia, wife of the giant Tsar Alexander III.

In her turn the Empress, who according to Marsden also believed in the efficacy of the mysterious herb, not only gave her financial help but something more important in Russia; a letter recommending whoever it might concern to render her every assistance in visiting hospitals and leper settlements. That there were no leper settlements in the proper sense of the word either in Yakutia or on the way to it did not detract from its value. With its help, and that of the Countess Alexandrine Tolstoy, Lady in Waiting to the Empress, she was able to enlist the aid of the Governor of Moscow, the Inspector of Moscow, the Bishop of Ufa (who had himself spent forty years of his life working as a missionary in Yakutia) and a number of other influential persons.

Yakutia, for which she was destined, was, and still is, a place of extremes. Covering almost 1,200,000 square miles of tundra and coniferous forest, it is part of the Forest of Forests, which in the USSR alone amounts to a quarter of the entire forest area of the world.

But what really distinguishes Yakutia is its extremes of climate. In winter temperatures often sink to −72F and at two places, Verkhoyansk and Oymakon, known as the 'Poles of Cold', −90.4F has been recorded. In Yakutia, when the temperature falls to −58F, a point at which machinery breaks, iron rods snap and an unpleasant phenomenon occurs in which the breath freezes, producing a crackling noise known as the 'whispering of the stars', they close the schools.

It is therefore not surprising that in Yakutia there is permafrost in many places to a depth of 1000 feet, in some places to more than 4200 feet: on the other hand, houses built on this seemingly rocklike medium generate enough heat to thaw the surface sufficiently to turn it into a quagmire in which they sink to their windowsills, sometimes capsizing completely.

In summer, the season Kate Marsden arrived there, the temperature zooms up to around 100F, which gives Verkhoyansk the honour of having the greatest temperature variation in the world, 192 degrees F, from −94 to 98F.

The capital of Yakutia is Yakutsk, one of the oldest towns in Siberia, founded by Cossack fur trappers in 1632. It stands on the banks of the Lena, a river 2680 miles long with a hydra-headed delta on the Arctic Ocean which rises five miles from Lake Baikal. Navigable for 2400 miles, its delta is frozen for all but three months of the year.

It was for this, even to Russians, little known region that Kate Marsden set off early in 1891, at the height of the Russian winter. She was accompanied by an Ada Field, of whom we learn next to nothing in the book, except that she was ill much of the time and had to be sent back to Moscow. They travelled by train to Zlatoust in the Chelyabinsk region of the Southern Urals, and there transferred to horse-drawn sledges for the long journey across the steppes to Krasnoyarsk, more than 2250 miles to the east.

At Zlatoust they—one assumed Field must have been similarly clad—dressed themselves in quantities of clothing that even the Siberians must have thought extraordinary: Jaeger undervests, 'loose kinds of bodies lined with flannel', three topcoats, eiderdown ulsters, full-length sheepskin coats and, on top of these, reindeer skin coats, long-haired hunting stockings and two sorts of felt boots, all of which made them so heavy and immobile that they had to be thrown into their equipages by the policemen who were seeing them off.

Among their principal provisions for the journey (Marsden appears to have been a rather erratic shopper) were 40 lbs of plum pudding and enough oil wicks to last for ten years. The route they followed for most of the way to Irkutsk was what foreigners called the Great Siberian Post Road and Russians called the *Trakt*. The *Trakt* extended from Perm in the Urals to Irkutsk and beyond to the Tsar's great silver mines at Nerchinsk in Transbaikalia, more than 3000 miles. Deep in snow, mud or dust according to the season, it was exactly as it always had been, apart from having been widened to twenty-one feet in the eighteenth century. This was the only road across Siberia, and that ended at Nerchinsk.

Along it posting stations were located at intervals of between ten and twenty miles. They were two-roomed log cabins, too small for the number of travellers and drivers they were called upon to accommodate and extremely dirty. They were, however, havens of rest compared with the *étapes*, the stockaded stations and the *polu étapes*, the intermediate stations built at intervals of between twenty-five and forty miles along the *Trakt*. Most foreigners travelling this road in the 1860s and '70s and until the railway was built were on their way to Peking by way of Mongolia, the only destination east of the Urals worth the expenditure of so much time and money. Travelling without intermission, London–St Petersburg–Peking took about fifty days. The fastest travellers were the imperial couriers between Peking and St Petersburg. Before the telegraph was built linking the two capitals, they frequently covered the 3618 miles between Irkutsk and St Petersburg in sixteen days, with 212 changes of horses, eating and sleeping in their sleighs, and averaging ten miles an hour for almost 400 consecutive hours!

There were three principal forms of conveyance: the *telega*, a springless, one-horse cart fitted with a leather hood and curtain for bad weather; the *kibitka*, similarly equipped, but which could also be converted into a horse-drawn sleigh; and the *tarantass*, the vehicle used by Marsden when the spring thaw began at Krasnoyarsk on the Yenisei river, a sort of hooded and, except for the driver, seatless basket about seven feet long supported on a couple of long flexible poles mounted on the four axle trees which acted as springs. It was drawn by a *troika*, a team of shaggy Siberian horses. In it the occupants travelled prone on their belongings which acted as shock absorbers: all these sorts of vehicle were driven by a *yamschick* (driver).

Until the Trans-Siberian Railway was completed to the river

Ob in 1895, Tyumen, used by the two women as a stopover, was the place where emigrants and exiles travelling to Omsk and points eastward of it in the warm weather waited for the horrible iron barges, towed by paddle-steamers carrying fare-paying passengers which conveyed them to Tomsk by way of various river systems. It was in a similar vessel that Marsden spent three weeks travelling down the Lena on her way to Yakutsk where the next stage of her journey was to begin, a 2000-mile horseback ride which was to take her into the horrible wilderness on the banks of the Vilyuy river, westwards from Yakutsk, where the lepers lived.

What do we think of Kate Marsden after reading her book? What do we know about her, beyond the fact that she was as indefatigable a lobbyist as she was a traveller, and that, in her own words, she took many backward steps and turned away from Christ at some period after the Russo-Turkish War—a memory fraught with the keenest regret? Very little. We know that she is enamoured, or aims to give the impression that she is, of the rich and royal—the least interesting parts of her book are those in which letters from 'personages' are reprinted, as are those from authorities testifying to her courage and persistence; but her aim was to raise funds to build hospitals, and without patronage very little could be accomplished in Russia, or anywhere else for that matter in 1891.

But it is difficult to gauge what was accomplished. We don't know if a hospital was ever built, nor or if this was a turning-point in the lives of the Lepers of Siberia? What did Marsden do subsequently? Did she ever go to India? Did she continue fund raising from the rich and powerful in comparative comfort far from the Vilvuy river? Did she ever find the herb? She doesn't tell us. And, given the lack of any information about her, it seems unlikely that we will ever know the answers to many of these questions.

Eric Newby

CONTENTS.

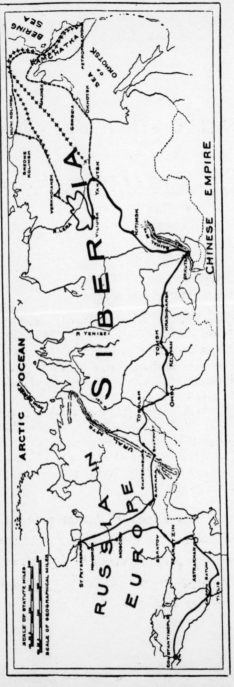

ON SLEDGE AND HORSEBACK

TO THE

OUTCAST SIBERIAN LEPERS.

———◆◆◆———

CHAPTER I.

CLEARING THE WAY.

The writer's object—Kindness of Her Imperial Majesty the Empress of Russia—The herb, reputed to arrest the progress of leprosy—A life-mission—Christ's lepers—"No remedy"—Efforts to relieve the sufferings of lepers—"Shoot them!"—The claims of religion and humanity—Lepers in the East—What people think—Arrival in Moscow—The "Golden-Headed City"—Prince Dolgoroukow—Journeys to St. Petersburg, and the gift of the Empress—Work in Moscow—Noble-minded Russians—Newspaper exaggerations—Kindness from high and low—Misunderstood—Taken for a spy—Fast friends—Clouds clear away—"A pleasure trip"—My outfit—Mounting the sledge—Off.

IT is with devout thankfulness to Almighty God that, after more than twelve months' travel, and almost constant exposure to perils of many kinds during that period, I am at length permitted to send forth this book. I seek not sympathy for hardship and pain, voluntarily undergone, or praise for any work partly accomplished. It is my earnest desire that all sympathy aroused may be directed to the suffering lepers, and not to me, and all praise to Him who has enabled a feeble woman to set her hand to a work which was waiting to be done. Had I consulted merely my own feelings, these pages would have contained only a simple record of the condition and wants of the lepers, and what is now being attempted to alleviate their misery. But I knew the particulars of the inconveniences, dangers, and exciting incidents, which have been, as it were, the inseparable companions of my travels, would add largely to the general interest of the book, and would therefore increase its sale. Let every purchaser remember that he is doing something, though only a trifle, to help the least cared-for members of the human race.

I desire, also, to acknowledge my great indebtedness to Her Imperial Majesty the Empress of Russia, without whose most prompt, valuable, and kind assistance it would have been utterly impossible either to carry on or to initiate this mission to the lepers of Siberia. Her Majesty's letter instructed all Government officials in the places I proposed to visit to give me every possible assistance. No royal lady could have entered with more readiness and sympathy into the philanthropic proposals submitted to Her Majesty.

The Empress confirmed the report which I had heard

both in Constantinople and Tiflis of the existence of a herb which was said to alleviate the sufferings caused by leprosy, and, in some cases, to remove the disease. I was also told that the herb was to be found in the far-off Yakutsk province of Siberia, where there were many lepers; but, being so jealously kept a secret by the natives, no one who wished to make experiments with it from mercenary motives could hope to obtain any information. But would the natives disclose the secret to one who wished only to benefit lepers throughout the Russian Empire, and wherever they existed in various parts of the world? Could they be persuaded to reveal all they knew to a woman who came to them for the sake of humanity, and on behalf of Christ? Some doctors, so I understood, had not cared to risk health and life, and others had neither the time nor the money to spend months and perhaps years in investigating the matter, visiting the lepers in isolated regions, and testing the properties of the herb in a systematic way.

My first acquaintance with the ravages of the frightful disease arose during the Russo-Turkish war. Since then, except during the period when I took many backward steps and turned away from Christ—a memory ever fraught with the keenest regret—the main subject of my thoughts has been the wants of the lepers and how to relieve them. The emotions aroused by the sight of two poor, mutilated, and helpless Bulgarians cannot be fully described. Before this time the conviction had taken hold upon me that my mission in life was to minister to those who received the smallest attention and care of all God's creatures. I had seen and heard of disease and suffering enough amongst the poor of my own country and amongst the victims of war. But they were within close reach, at least, of abundant Christian and philanthropic efforts. But the lepers in the far-off uncivilised regions of the world—who cared for them ? What medical attention did they receive ? what tender ministration from the gentle hand of woman soothed their sufferings ? Cut off from their fellow-creatures, avoided, despised, and doomed to a living death—surely these, of all afflicted people, ought to become the object of my mission. Debarred from intercourse with others, except with those who suffered in a similar way, deprived of the comforts of civilisation, left without proper nourishment, and outcasts from the consolation of religion, the lepers seemed to me to demand, in a special and unique manner, human aid. They were emphatically Christ's lepers, since so few of Christ's servants, in proportion to the needs of lepers, had, as yet, been able to devote themselves to their relief.

"No remedy—no relief !" A thousand times have those mournful words racked my thoughts and pained my heart. Whilst science, philanthropy and religion were busily engaged in devising means for relieving

pain, curing disease, and consoling the sufferer, could
nothing be done for Christ's lepers?   Often and often
the wish was uppermost in my heart, Would to God
that the Healer and Saviour of men were amongst the
lepers of to-day, to give the loving command, " I
will, be thou clean."

Before long I learned, with much satisfaction, that,
in many parts of the world, hospitals were erected, and
medical and nursing aid provided for the relief of
lepers.   But I learned, at the same time, that in other
parts they were shamefully neglected, and abandoned
by the rest of the community in which they had dwelt.
With many conflicting testimonies before me, I
determined to see for myself the true state of matters,
taking no report at second-hand.

My desire to set out on this investigation was
intensified on hearing from some pessimistic and inhuman quarters that the best remedy for such an incurable and loathsome malady was—*murder*.   " Shoot
them—poison them—anything to put them out of
their misery ! "   My blood recoiled at such a
" method," as, indeed, would be the case with anyone
possessing the true love of humanity ; and I firmly
resolved to use every means in my power, with Divine
assistance, to discover a remedy, and, if such efforts
failed, to devise efficient methods for alleviating the
miseries which accompanied the disease, and for
bringing all lepers under the humane as well as the

religious influence of the servants of the Gospel of Jesus Christ.

Before proceeding to Siberia to discover the herb, and endeavour to bring its remedial qualities within the reach of all lepers throughout the world, I proposed to visit the East, and acquaint myself with the condition of the lepers in that quarter.

At Jerusalem, although many of the lepers receive the best attention that medical skill and nursing aid can contrive, I saw enough misery to strengthen my resolution. At Constantinople the scene of horror appalled me, and I longed, with a fervency that cannot be described, for the swift help of Heaven and of men in my mission of relief. I may be called an enthusiast, or a woman who bids high for the world's applause. I care not what I am called, or what I am thought of, so long as the goal of my ambition be reached, or so long as I may see before I die that the work commenced, though faultily, is on its way to completion.

Travelling across the Black Sea and the Caucasus from Constantinople, I arrived at Moscow in November 1890. Any one who has been travelling through a strange country for two or three days and nights without stopping, and ignorant of the language of the natives, will easily understand my feelings of relief when I was at last told that the next station was Moscow, especially if my reader is tall, and has

experienced that awkward position of being cramped
for a long time in a railway carriage.

The train stopped ; and having collected my many
wraps, I got out, and at once confronted a true Mos-
covite winter, which my English clothing, notwithstanding the above-mentioned rugs, was ill-fitted to
face. Once in the sledge and on my way to the hotel,
I almost forgot the intense cold in my eagerness to
notice everything I passed. The number of churches
especially attracted me as I drove through the quaint
narrow streets, uphill and down. The sledge gliding
along noiselessly over the snow, and the horses not
having bells, the driver has to shout to warn the people
to get out of the way. In a thickly-populated place
like Moscow, it needs a great amount of care to avoid
being run over, especially as most people have very
high fur collars which reach far above their ears, so
that they are almost deaf to everything.

Moscow is rightly called the "golden-headed city,"
owing to the number of golden domes ornamenting her
churches, though some are painted blue and others
green. Some of the domes, I was told, are covered with
thin sheets of real gold, the rest of the church being
painted white, picked out with lavender. All these
different colours present a very brilliant and beautiful
appearance, particularly when the sun shines upon them.

My first step was to go the Governor, Prince
Dolgoroukow, who represents His Imperial Majesty the

Czar. The etiquette at such audiences is to appear in full day dress. Happily, I had my nurse's uniform with me, which suits all occasions. So I brushed it up, and, with a clean pair of white strings to my somewhat worn bonnet, I concluded my toilette, and finally set out, not without a feeling of nervousness, which unfortunately I can seldom shake off.

Arriving at the palace, I was soon ushered into the presence of the Prince, who, by his kind manner and gentle voice, at once banished every uncomfortable feeling. "What can I do for you?" he asked. Then I told him about my mission, asking his permission to visit the hospitals of the city, and any lepers to be found in it. His kind face took a still kinder expression as he drew closer, and questioned me about my proposed work, seeming rather bewildered that any woman should attempt it. He then summoned the Inspector of Hospitals, and gave orders to show me every place I might wish to see. As I rose to depart he presented me with his beautifully-bound book on Moscow, a gift which I then took as a great favour, but now, since the kind Prince has passed away, I treasure as a loving remembrance of one who, though advanced in age, readily exerted himself on behalf of the poor, suffering lepers.

The next day I began to work in earnest, calling upon everyone I could think of who might help in the work. At first all went well; but, before long, difficulties began to crop up. Twice I went to St. Petersburg, a journey which takes twelve hours. The kindness and assistance so willingly bestowed by Her Imperial Majesty, the Empress, has been acknowledged; but I have not yet mentioned that Her Imperial Majesty sent me a thousand roubles (about £100) to help forward the mission. The Countess Alexandrine Tolstoi, whose warm and motherly reception I shall never forget, also did everything in her power to further my plans. There were many others, too, who seconded my efforts.

Let those who trust to exaggerated and unfavourable newspaper reports, and are under the delusion that little good can come out of Russia, bear in mind that there are numbers of noble men and women in the country always ready to stretch out the hand of fellow-ship to anyone coming in the Master's name to help His sick and suffering ones. Let such persons pause before judging a whole nation by mere hearsay accounts. When we think of the enormous extent of the Russian territory, of the different races inhabiting it, each having a separate language, and some of them not knowing Russian at all—a fact which in itself is a serious obstacle in the progress of civilisation—then the strong opinions formed concerning deficiencies, evils, and abuses must be modified by a spirit of forbearance and justice. During a personal experience of, altogether, two years I have had many opportunities of studying the Russian people, especially as I have mixed in almost all classes of society ; and I most gladly state that, with but very few exceptions, high and low have treated me with never-failing kindness and courtesy. Nay, more, some of the highest have opened a loving mother's arms to me when in trouble ; and my rough soldier's tender care all through my journey will be an ever-grateful and cherished memory.

My work in Moscow in arousing interest and collecting funds was beset with difficulties. I fully stated my plans—namely, to find the herb. But, in spite of my plainness of speech (unfortunately, I could not speak a word of the Russian tongue), my motives were misconstrued, and all kinds of rumours were set afloat. Because I stayed at an hotel, some people became suspicious, and looked at me askance. On arriving in Moscow, many of the English residents spontaneously opened their doors to me, and seemed to take a great interest in my work. But, one day, an article appeared in a London journal containing a reference to me, and written by a well-meaning but unwise friend ; and then, laughable as it may seem, I was suspected of being a political spy. It was no laughing matter, however, to me, for friends began to keep aloof, and I became uncomfortably conscious of being decidedly under a cloud. It was not pleasant either to drive about in a little open sledge in a temperature about 20° below zero (Fahrenheit), the wind and snow driving full in one's face, with clothes (except

a shouba lent by a kind friend) only suitable for
an English climate.

Though certainly a little depressed, yet by no
means did I give way to despair. There was one
never-failing source of comfort and encouragement;
and, bowing humbly and pleadingly at that Divine
source, my heart became recharged with hope, and
the silver lining of the cloud grew more distinct
and real. Then, too, the few English and the many
Russian friends who remained steadfast were, in truth,
a rock of comfort when the days were darkest. Some
of these dear friends even sent food to the hotel, and
nursed me in illness; but their love of perfect pri-
vacy prevents me mentioning them by name. Others,
however, I am free to mention. General and Madame
Costanda, Princess Gagarine, and my unfailing friend
and companion, Miss Ada Field, stood by me un-
flinchingly. We all met and discussed matters fully.
We decided to go again to Prince Dolgoroukow to seek
his help and advice. He offered to assist us in every
way, but, in a few days, fell ill; and so our hopes were
again dashed to the ground.

But we were too ready to " fret," for we found that
the good Prince, notwithstanding physical weakness,
was working amongst his friends. Madame Costanda
also worked hard amongst hers; the Princess Gagarine
wrote a splendid article in the *Moscow Gazette;* the
German daily papers discussed the matter; new and

unexpected English and Russian friends sprang up in all directions. Although some could only give their mite to the funds, all gave their sympathy and prayers. So the cloud gradually broke up and drifted away.

Letters of introduction were obtained to influential persons in Siberia, including one from the Bishop of Ufa, whom I had visited at Ufa, and who had worked as a missionary for forty years amongst the Yakuts. Stores were bought, clothes made, and in a few weeks everything was ready for this perilous, long, and unknown journey. What am I saying—a perilous journey?— nay, some people said I was going to take a "pleasure trip." So let it be. I plead guilty to the soft impeachment on the one condition that all ladies who give this seductive term to my journey will undertake to start from the vicinity of Moscow on the first of February next year, and follow precisely the same route that the writer took, travel by the same conveyances that carried her, stop at the same places where she halted, carry the same luggage that accompanied her, and, above all, witness the same sights, and see the identical people that crowd to her memory to-day. Happy should I be could I offer " personal conductorship; " but this is impossible. I fear the lady tourists will be unable to find me, being due in the hospitable regions of Kamschatka somewhere about the date of their departure from Moscow.

To assist the lady tourist, and, I hope, to interest the reader, a few details of my stores and outfit shall here be given. When we came to consider such matters there was quite a titillation of excitement; and I really believe that some of my younger friends felt almost as if they were preparing for a wedding. Even my own attention, I must confess, was diverted from the lepers for a moment in thinking what to wear, what provisions to take, whether we should have a sound sledge, and a sober and trustworthy driver, or whether we should be called to experience the many tales told about the tipsy driver, for ever sipping his dear vodka, and having no qualms of conscience in landing the traveller topsy-turvy some dark night in the depths of a forest, or in the solemn stillness of a snow-drift. I am afraid, however, that I frequently irritated my friends when, in the midst of discussing things to wear and things to eat, I went off at a tangent to speak of the far-off lepers, and what they wanted.

Of course, it was quite natural for the gentlemen to remark that, like most of my sex, I wanted to get at the end of the journey before setting off. If there was any amusing oasis in a desert of anxiety, from starting from London in 1890 to returning thither in 1892, it was surely the excitement created by these final preparations for packing off the " tourists." As to food, everybody was eager to suggest something that combined keeping qualities with those of tastiness. Con

sequently, tinned and potted meats and fish, and bottled
fruits, and so on, were mentioned in wondrous variety.
But, after all, it was decided that we need only take a
few boxes of sardines, biscuits, some bread, tea, and one
or two other trifles, which included forty pounds of plum-
pudding! This delicious compound would certainly
"keep" in cold weather, as all housewives know; and
I liked it, and so was persuaded to take it as the staple
article of the journey. A dear English lady friend
offered and provided it. We expected to find opportunities in the villages (the Moscow side of Yakutsk,
at least) for replenishing our larder, so why bother
about a load of eatables ?

Then there were other necessary articles to be stowed
away. Somebody said that those little oil-wicks, used
instead of night-lights, were not to be had for love or
money in Siberia ; so I got two dozen boxes, and then
was calmly told that I had enough to last for ten years.
Another English friend gave me forty pounds of candles ;
but, by-and-bye, as I may as well mention here, on
coming to unpack the stores, I found that only four
pounds had been allowed to remain intact. About the
clothing—well, that was a decided burden in more ways
than one. I had a whole outfit of Jaeger garments,
which I prized more and more as the months went on ;
then a loose kind of body, lined with flannel, a very
thickly-wadded eider-down ulster, with sleeves long
enough to cover the hands entirely, the fur collar

reaching high enough to cover the head and face. Then a sheep-skin reaching to the feet, and furnished with a collar which came over the fur one. Then over the sheep-skin I had to wear a *dacha*, which is a fur coat of reindeer skin. It was not surprising that, when thus accoutred, broadened, and lengthened by a great many inches, I failed to recognise K. M. in the looking-glass, which a laughing girl held up before me.

But I have not yet finished; some other articles have still to be described. A long thick pair of Jaegar stockings made of long hair; over them a pair of gentlemen's thickest hunting stockings; over them a pair of Russian boots made of felt, coming high up over the knee; and over them a pair of brown felt *valenkies*. Then I was provided with a large fur bag or sack into which I could step; my head-covering was a fur-lined cap, and the et-ceteras consisted of shawls, rugs, and wraps. All this immense load of wool, and fur, and skins to cover a bit of frail and feeble humanity! Yet there was not an ounce too much, as after-experience proved.

We went by train to Zlatoust (a few hundred miles from Moscow), whence we were to start in the sledge, and commence my memorable journey through Siberia.

At Zlatoust the head of the police met us in full state, with about twenty policemen; the colonel of the mounted police was also present, as well as the station-master, and a crowd of villagers. It was, I need scarcely say, the letter of the Empress that caused all this attention and deference. The honour accorded was, of course, to Her Majesty, and not to me. The difficulties of mounting the sledge, in my loaded and hampered condition, I had not contemplated; but now, on seeing the conveyance at the door, my heart sank, and I longed for some good fairy to waft me gently from the station into the corner of the sledge. But it was of no use to give way to heart-sinking, or to long for impossibilities.

That sledge—one of the elevated kind, standing a long way from the ground—had to be mounted. The feat must be accomplished somehow. How I managed to walk, or totter, down the steps of the station without an accident is a marvel. Having got over that portion of the feat, I stood at the side of the sledge trying to solve the knotty problem of how to get in. There was no step to help me; and there was the crowd of men, women, and children gazing at me. What was I to do? I tried to take in the humour of the situation, which was probably the wisest thing to do under the circumstances. Three muscular policemen attempted to lift me gently into the sledge; but their combined strength was futile under the load. So they had to set me on the ground again. Then I attempted, in a kind of majestic, contemptuous way to mount without assistance; but, alas! my knees would *not* bend. My pride had to succumb; I was helpless. Two policemen came and essayed another manœuvre. They took me by the arms and then, at their signal, I made one desperate, frantic effort, and I was in.

But " what a falling off," to be sure ! For one, who was known to have come with a letter from the Empress—the importance of which can only be truly fathomed by a Russian—to be quizzed and stared at by the crowd whilst engaged in these undignified operations ! But all was not yet over. I was in, but I had to be packed and stowed away. The men pushed, and pulled, and dragged, and coaxed ; and, at last, I and my clothes were considered ready for starting. As to bowing and thanking my assistants, that was impossible ; I just sat, and fairly gasped, and longed to get away. My friend, Miss Field, underwent an ordeal somewhat similar to that which I had endured ; the driver and the soldier took their seats ; and then we were off.

CHAPTER II.

FIRST EXPERIENCES ON THE ROAD.

The pleasures of sledging along a broken-up road—Wolves—A
cheap "hotel"—Frozen lakes—"Survival of the fittest"—
Village dwellings—Patient cows—A chivalrous soldier—
Ekaterinberg prison—Irbit Fair—A chaotic sledge-ride—
"Pirate" drivers—A feather bed at last—Tjumen hospital—
A reading and writing potentate—Roses in Siberia—A model
farm—A polluted river, and what the people thought of it—
The peasants' love for the Empress—A petition to the
Empress—Farewell to English hospitality.

OUR experience of sledging along a road terribly broken
up, owing to the immense traffic and almost endless
string of sledges, carrying heavy loads of goods to the
annual Siberian fair, held in February, will be repeated
in your case, dear reader, if you ever undertake a similar
journey to Siberia at a corresponding period. Bump, jolt,
bump, jolt—over huge frozen lumps of snow and into
holes, and up and down those dreadful waves and fur-
rows, made by the traffic— such is the stimulating motion
you will have to submit to for a few thousand miles.
Your head seems to belong to every part of the sledge;
it is first bumped against the top; then the conveyance
gives a lurch, and you get an unexpected knock against

the side; then you cross one of the ruts, and, first, you are thrown violently forward against the driver, and, second, you just as quickly rebound. This sort of motion is all very well for a few miles; but after a time it gets too monotonously trying. You ache from head to foot; you are bruised all over; your poor brain throbs until you give way to a kind of hysterical outcry; your head-gear gets displaced; your temper, naturally, becomes slightly ruffled, and you are ready to gasp, from so frequently clutching at the sides to save yourself.

Added to all this is the constant yelling of the driver, who thinks it one of the paramount duties of his calling to make a noise above the ringing of the sledge bells. So you go on merrily, the horses dashing along like the steeds in a fire-engine, or like the hot-blooded beauties of Phæthon. The yelling of your Jehu increases in volume when you tear through villages, alarming poor folk, who clear off, helter-skelter, pell-mell, with knitted brows and muttered observations. All the dogs, roused from their peaceful pursuits, surround you, forming a lively escort, barking, growling, fighting, and jumping snappishly at the horses' heads. Night comes on apace, to soften your feelings with a lowered temperature and the pleasing suggestions that darkness brings. Still on you merrily go—but, oh, for five minutes' peace! Bumping, jolting, tossing; heaved, pitched and thumped. Bright memories of asphalt, blockwood, and penny omnibuses spring up to diversify your thoughts. Little gleams of light which you pass on your way seem to come from tiny hut windows in the forest.

"Driver" (Yemstchick), shouts your companion, "can't we stop a minute at one of those huts?"

"Eh, what, madam?" (Tchevo Barienya?)

"Those huts where the lights are—can't we rest there?"

"Lights? They're wolves" (Eto seriae poshli).

"Oh!"

You know you can't go faster, or you would certainly urge the driver to quicken the pace. Warily you try to peep round to see if those little gleaming eyes are close at the rear. And now your Jehu makes a mighty spurt. Slash, slash, goes the whip; thud, thud, go the reins on the horses' flanks. "Little doves; little sisters," are the coaxing epithets the man addresses to the tired creatures, mixed with his wild yells. You have a vague idea that the appointed place for halting cannot be far distant. Jehu begins to want his vodka; you long for the sight of the singing samovar,* and a nice snug warm room, with feather bed, well-aired sheets, and, perhaps, a warming-pan; and the horses seem to sniff their supper from afar, so on they wildly go, snorting and foaming, until, at last, at the post-station you pull up sharp.

You are then, in a semi-comatose state, dragged from

* The samovar is a kind of urn, with charcoal underneath for heating the water.

the sledge; and, on gaining a footing, you feel more like a battered old log of mahogany than a gently-nurtured Englishwoman.

And now, dear reader, let me introduce you to your somewhat primitive "hotel"; but have patience. The key must first of all be found, and then candles and matches. Have your pocket-handkerchief ready, if you can find it, and place it close to your nostrils the moment the door is opened. The hinges creak; and your first greeting is a gust of hot, fœtid air, which almost sends you back; but you remember the cold outside and the cravings of hunger, and so you go in.

The *menu* is regulated entirely according to your own tastes; in fact, it consists chiefly of the viands which you have brought with you, and which do not happen to have bounced out of the sledge, or which you haven't flung to the wolves on your way. You will be badly off indeed if you cannot contrive to have a few dry biscuits and a glass of tea. There are no waiters to bother you at this hotel, and no fees of any kind; and that should relieve your mind.

The sheep-skin and rugs (none of the cleanest) are then laid in the middle of the floor. That is your bed; but don't suppose you will have sole possession of it. One glance around the walls at the numbers of moving specks upon them of different sizes and families will at once dispel that illusion, whilst the probable arrival of another tardy traveller will deprive you of even the comfort of a room to yourself.

The heat of these premises is grateful and comforting at first; but, some hours before dawn, you long for the intense cold outside, and you register a vow that never as long as you live will you enter such a stifling hole again. But, alas for human constancy! the very next night, or perhaps for many nights, you will eagerly seek the shelter of one of these warm structures, and sleep soundly, until awakened by a sensation of approaching suffocation.

What is known as the short cut from Zlatoust to Ekaterinberg a good deal resembles an Irishman's mile. On being asked how long his mile was the Irishman replied, " For sure, 'tis a mile and a half, your honour ; but maybe 'tis longer if ye wish it."

The dense forests on the road look grand and stately, but sometimes our admiration of their sturdy growth received a sudden check by the appearance of a wolf. One brown specimen looked round and faced us, as if he meant to fight; but, on second thoughts, he turned tail and slowly ambled off. Then we saw a black one crouching at the foot of a tree ; but he, too, made no attempt to molest us.

Sometimes we came to a large lake, which we had to glide over, meeting, now and then, a few men, who had cut holes in the lake, and were lying on the ice, fishing. Russian peasants sit and recline on blocks of ice, as if

they were feather beds ; and little children, with one
skirt round their bodies, and a handkerchief on their
heads, but with no fur of any kind, run about when
there are 20° of frost (Reaumur), and sit placidly on
heaps of snow. The cold of Russia has one decided
effect: it finds out the weakest young people, and kills
them off before they reach manhood or womanhood ;
so that weak and delicate men and women are seldom
met with, at least, in country districts.

We passed several dirty villages, having broad
streets, and on either side wooden houses, made of the
trunks of trees, plastered round thickly with stable
refuse. Although this simple method has the advan
tage of shutting out the wind and frost, it also shuts in
all the foul smells. It is a marvel how these villagers
can contrive to exist, and bring up families in such unwholesome dwellings. As to the cows, from which the
people derive their chief nourishment, they are as quiet
and as patient as the peasants themselves. They
always seem to be in one's way when passing through
a village, and endure, with the utmost equanimity, a
sudden collision with the sledge, or the sharp crack of
the driver's whip.

On arriving at Ekaterinberg, we found accommodation at the excellent American hotel, the best hotel
that I came across on this journey. The servants here
are a model to their race, for they do not swarm around
for fees on the traveller's departure.

The head of the police, Baron Taube, is a perfect specimen of a fine Russian, full of energy and spirit, with the most delicate appreciation of the courtesy due to ladies, especially those who are put under his care. He gave me a soldier, named Popoff, who proved a worthy representative of his master. When we came to post-houses it was often a problem with me, weighted and hampered as I was with so many clothes and wraps, how to scramble out of the sledge without assistance; but this man stretched out his hands, and I just tumbled into them, furs and all. He took my arm, led me up the rickety steps, removed my furs and high boots, and then stood still, with a look on his serious face that plainly meant, "What more can I do?" Sometimes he stood and saluted, saying, "Slushayous" (I am obeying your orders). His delicate attention and anxiety to serve me would have touched any woman. After taking his meals, consisting generally of black bread and scraps, he always came into my room saying, "I humbly thank you." Yes, I do love those enduring, hard-working, splendid Russian soldiers; I would trust that one with my life any day.

The prison at Ekaterinberg is not one of the best of its kind. It appeared to me badly lighted, badly ventilated, and badly kept. This was my first prison experience; and a shiver went through my heart when, on entering the prison, the grating noise of bolts and locks told of the many poor fellows doomed to be shut in from the world. Soldiers stood with their guns and bayonets ready to quell an outbreak. The rattling of the prisoners' chains, which extend from waist to ankles, is a sound one never forgets. In the yard were several prisoners, with the snow piled up around them, and wearing clothes too scanty to keep them warm, even on an autumn day in England. The frightened look on some, the despairing look on others, and the scowl on the faces of a few, produced a train of thought, calling up in imagination varied pictures in the past lives of these men.

The room where the prisoners took their meals was dirty, and badly ventilated. The food was contained in a large wooden bowl placed on the table; each man had a spoon, which he dipped into the bowl and passed to his mouth. The unwholesome condition of the room, the soup spilt on the table, and those dirty wooden ladles made me wonder whether any prison in my own country could show such a scene. The head warder informed me that, although the prison was built to hold only a specified number of prisoners, yet, in the summer, it often contained two or three times as many.

Whilst in Ekaterinberg we came across some English friends, Messrs. Yates and Wardroper, and the agent of the British and Foreign Bible Society. It was these gentlemen, for whose kind help I am much indebted, who suggested that we should go to the Irbit

Fair. They believed that a merchant from Yakutsk would be there, who would give me valuable information about the lepers. This fair is held annually during February. Merchants come from all parts of the Empire, bringing with them all kinds of commodities. For the number of nationalities represented, for the babel of tongues, and the vast heterogeneous assortment of goods displayed, this assemblage is probably without a match in the world. The fair is opened by the priests with a religious ceremony, and is the only thing that keeps Irbit alive; for the rest of the year it is almost a deserted and forgotten place.

We made the journey to Irbit, of one hundred miles, by sledge, and found accommodation in a room, which contained a bedstead but no bedding, two crazy chairs, one dilapidated table, and the usual unwelcome occupants. The merchant from Yakutsk was discovered, and, when told of the mission to his district by a woman, positively refused to believe the statement, in view of the almost insurmountable difficulties it entailed. He was quietly told that the woman in question had "laid help upon One that was mighty," and was not relying upon herself outside of God. When, however, his doubts were removed, he devoutly made the sign of the cross, saying that he would pray for a blessing to rest on the work and the worker. He told me all he knew about the lepers, but had no information to give about the herb.

It was here that, by the advice and with the assistance of the English friends, already mentioned, I bought
a sledge, as it was cheaper to travel in one of my own
than having a fresh one at every stage.

The ride from Irbit to Tjumen was, I think, the
worst bit of sledging I ever experienced. Some of the
holes that we had to get through, or over, were positively
dreadful. The driver actually had to pull up now and
then and dismount, in order to see how deep the next
hole was. We expected almost every minute that
horses and driver, soldier, ladies and all, would be
mixed up in dire chaotic confusion. That, hundred
miles of shaking and bumping down holes and up holes,
and over huge lumps of snow that looked like the
remains of ancient buildings, so wearied and dazed us
that, I believe, on arriving at Tjumen we were more
dead than alive.

But we were to have other experiences along this
portion of the journey. An incident occurred which
threatened to put us in a very awkward predicament.
The driver, quite a young man, happened to be what
is called a "free" driver, in distinction from Government drivers. Being a free driver, he had some
of the rights and privileges which the drivers of
"pirate" omnibuses so provokingly assume. These
drivers were not bound to take the Government road ;
they went by any route or track they chose, provided
the "fares" did not forcibly prevent them. It was our

wish to call at a certain village, where we knew a
tolerably good lodging for the night could be obtained.
Our man at first mildly protested. When we became
aware, by jolting over by-roads and no roads at all,
that he was following his own inclination, we expostu-
lated. Then he flatly refused to follow our wishes, and
said he was going to another village, which, according
to the soldier, was fully eight miles out of the way.

"I sha'n't charge you anything extra," said he, with
brazen-faced impudence.

"But we don't want you to make us a present of the
eight miles. We insist on going where you are ordered
to take us."

The fellow then became more obdurate, notwithstanding the soldier threatening all sorts of terrible
things. At last, throwing the reins on the horses'
backs, he dismounted, and came to the side of the
sledge. Remember, please, it was night, with a waste-
howling wilderness of snow all round, and no human
habitation within many miles.

"Look here," said he, "this is your sledge, and those are
my horses; if you don't want to go where I am driving
you to, I can just take out the horses and go home."

Here was a prospect for two benighted women—-to
find our way on foot into the Government road again,
tramping through unknown depths of snow, and then
walk on to the nearest post-station, or else remain in the
sledge all night by ourselves, whilst the soldier went off

for horses. The soldier, after another long, angry ex-
hortation, said something or other that seemed to bring
the man to his senses, for he remounted, shook the
reins, and dashed off in the direction we had ordered
him to take. On arriving at the village, the soldier
wanted to report the fellow for his misconduct. Then
came repentance. The " pirate " dropped on his knees,
grovelled on the ground, and begged and implored us to
forgive him. Then it came out that he was only obeying his master's orders, and that these free drivers have a
knavish way of taking the traveller by circuitous routes,
and charging for the extra distance. We let the youth
off, but vowed we would shun the pirates for ever after.

A pleasant surprise awaited us at Tjumen. Any
ladies undergoing so many hours of torture between
Irbit and Tjumen will derive some consolation from
the fact that a hearty English welcome is in store.
Mr. and Mrs. Wardroper received us at their house as
if we had been their own children. We sat down,
travel-stained, bruised, and ill, to a hot supper, and
were afterwards sent off for a night's rest. We tumbled
on to the soft and dainty bed just as we were, and soon
fell asleep. On awaking, a little reflection was necessary
before being able to realise our surroundings. What
had become of the sheep-skin, the dirty floor, the fœtid
air, the vermin, and the rest? Ah! indeed, Mr. Wardroper's house was a little heaven, compared to the places
where we had usually passed the nights.

Tjumen is an old town, with long, broad streets and
several churches, generally painted white, with green
domes, giving them a bright and fresh appearance. The
hospital, I am sorry to say, is the worst I have ever
seen. But then, of course, after my experience of clean,
bright English hospitals, I am of necessity a severe critic.
Want of cleanliness, ventilation, and good management
were everywhere apparent, and but few precautions
were taken to isolate infectious from other cases.

I accepted an invitation to visit a splendid estate
about forty miles from Tjumen. The roads on a portion
of the journey were so narrow that the horses had to
run "geese fashion"—two behind and one in front—
and sometimes tandem fashion. The sun shone full
into our faces, and the glaring light, combined with the
dazzling snow, had a strange effect. On closing our
eyes we saw black snow with bright dazzling silver
stars dotted all over.

In a room in one of the villages where we halted,
there were many pots of flowers, and large Chinese
roses, which at home would only grow in green-houses,
and yet here, in this terribly cold country, the rooms are
kept so hot, that in the better class of dwellings all
kinds of flowers may be found. We were received at
the estate with lavish hospitality by its owner, and were
surprised to find at such an outlandish place every kind
of European appliance for farming, cheese, and butter-
making. Being an English woman, I was naturally

pleased to see tempting butter once more, that had not been fingered and mauled about by dirty peasants. The cows were in splendid condition, though not of good breed. Their singular appearance almost gave me the idea of a shaggy Shetland pony and an English cow rolled into one. If an English farmer wants to win a prize at the Agricultural Show for extraordinary "points," all he has to do is to order one of these strange creatures.

Here but little interest is felt in the education of the people. It is a common thing to find but one man amongst two or three neighbouring villages who can read and write; and this man is quite a little potentate. If the governor of the province wants private information about any of the inhabitants, he sends to him, who, if unjust, has a capital opportunity for paying off old scores, and getting his enemy despatched to prison.

In the village next to the estate I was visiting, a school had just been built by the kind help of my hosts, who begged me to go and see it. In the midst of hearing the children read, an old man suddenly appeared on the scene, and begged to be allowed to speak to me. Seeing the red cross on the sledge, he thought I must be someone of consequence, and, therefore, came to implore me to do the villagers a service. He said the river was polluted by the refuse of a paper-mill ten miles away, and that the whole village was thereby being ruined.

I went off to the river, tasted and smelt the water, and found it was not fit for either man or beast. On returning to the village, a striking and unexpected scene awaited me. The people cried and implored me to help them, bowed down and pleaded, as I never knew people could plead, saying that the cattle refused to drink the water, that men, women, and children were ill from it, and that they had to walk four and six miles to the nearest village for every drop of water, unless they used melted snow, for men and cattle. They dreaded the summer, because that would mean death to them. The old men, with their heads bowed, the young ones, forgetting their village bashfulness in their excitement, appealing with their earnest faces, and the women uttering a piteous lament—all tried to make me fully understand by words and signs the vital importance of the matter. Some of the families had been 300 years in the village, and to remove to another place meant ruin and desolation to many. I wonder what English peasants would have done under similar circumstances, and with no one to help them. No, I don't wonder; I know what they would do first. The offending paper-mill would not have the chance of poisoning the water for another day. But here were some 300 people, apparently being ruined and starved by the despotic selfishness of one man, and they were all as powerless to help themselves as any baby.

I certainly had not come into Siberia to look after polluted rivers; but how could I refuse to listen to the touching appeal? I told them that I was going on to Tobolsk, where I would see the governor, and would plead with him on their behalf; and, should this prove insufficient, the case would be laid before a higher authority. I begged of them to make of this a special subject of prayer, as I was only a very helpless tool in the matter, and could do nothing unless God chose to use me for this purpose. They listened reverently, then bowed low, and said they would pray every day with all their hearts. My friend then asked me to show them a photograph of the Empress, which Her Majesty had so graciously given me, with her own signature; and to see them crowding round, peering shyly at the picture, some with open mouths, others in a reverent attitude, with uncovered heads, many with half-starved, weary faces, was a scene which would at least have pleased artistic eyes, and touched tender hearts at the Royal Academy. When I got into the sledge, all the people came bare-headed to shake hands, led by the father, or oldest man of the village. As I drove off, tears ran down their poor worn cheeks; and as they said " God bless you !" a pang of pain shot through my heart, and I prayed that our Lord would indeed enable me to help them.

Then we drove on to the paper-mill, about seven miles away. The cold was intense, with a strong wind. The

horses were quickly covered with frost; icicles hung
from their nostrils and mouths; the driver's whiskers
were soon frozen, and icicles hung from his moustache,
and also from my friend's veil. It was a long and
tiring drive, but those weary faces urged me on. At
the mill I found that the statement of the villagers was
only too true, for the chemicals used for washing filthy
rags were thrown into the river. The horses tore along
on our return, much to our delight, as by this time our
faces fairly ached with the cold. A warm welcome,
plenty of food, and the beloved *samovar*, did wonders,
and we were soon in a comfortable bed.

Early in the morning, a deputation arrived from the
two villages we had visited the day before with a petition for me to present, fully describing their position.
We hurried back to Tjumen, to start for Tobolsk, in
order to catch the Governor of Tobolsk before he
left, and speak to him about the polluted river, and
the condition of those poor people. The prison at
Tjumen, with all its wretchedness, is vividly impressed on my memory. Indeed, wherever one went on
this journey there was always something to harass the
feelings and rack the nerves, whilst the greatness of the
difficulties was enough to paralyse one's energies. It
is not wonderful that in such unwieldy dominions as
these, the doctrine of *laissez faire* opens so tempting a
vista to worried and overworked officials.

We packed up and went off. Mrs. Wardroper came

in her own sledge as far as the river to say good-bye; and as she stood there, wishing us God-speed, I wondered whether I should ever see another English face in this vast wild Siberia.

CHAPTER III.

MOSTLY MISHAPS.

Minor inconveniences—A specimen of " Young Siberia "—Russian harness—Shoeing horses—An accident—A smash—We are shot on to a river—Another accident—Those horses!—About post-stations and villagers—Tobolsk—Asking for the Word of Life—Safe at Tukalinsk—A *levée*—Visits to Tukalinsk prison— A pitiable sight—Convicts travelling in winter—A petition to " Her Highness "—Visit to a vagabond house.

THE horses dashed off full gallop, rushing through freshly formed snowdrifts. The snow soon found its way into every corner of the sledge, which, although covered at the top, was quite open in front. Then the snow had a way of settling down the collars of our coats, and, when melted by the heat of the body, trickling down the neck; and sometimes it flew up the sleeves unless we were careful to keep them closed at the wrists. Our good substantial boxes were all stowed away in the " hold "; over them was a layer of straw, and on the straw we sat, or, rather, reclined, with pillows at our backs. The word "reclined" suggests ease and comfort; but, when applied to sledge-travelling, under the circumstances that we travelled, it

means "Hobson's choice." You are compelled to put
yourself, or get put, into that position; and in that
position you must remain. The compulsory nature of
this reclining is apt to become rather trying to one of an
independent spirit, especially when that one has to submit to the inevitable for several hours together, and
with no possibility of getting a firm hold for the feet.
Some people fancy a sledge, in the way of the comfort
and ease which it offers, is like a nice roomy bath-chair.
Well, I won't argue the question; but I wish such people
could have seen us on this identical journey I am now
speaking of.

For six hours all went well, with the normal amount
of bumping and jolting. We had, this time, another
youthful driver, a rare specimen of "Young Siberia."
As darkness fell it appeared to us that he was getting
a little reckless; but we said nothing, attributing his
daring exploits to vodka, or to the bitter cold, or to the
faulty way of harnessing the horses. Anyhow, as midnight approached, it must be confessed that we became
slightly nervous and irritable, having our recent noc-
turnal adventure vividly before our minds. We had a
strong presentiment that something was going to happen. The harness, I must mention, is often responsible
for accidents in sledge travelling. One peculiarity
amongst Siberians is the obliviousness of the fact that
nature makes horses of various sizes; for the harness is
all of one regulation size. So you may see a horse ten

hands high with harness fit for one of fifteen hands, and *vice versâ*. The effect is often ludicrous, and sometimes painful to lovers of animals. People endowed with imagination would probably liken the small horses, with their large harness, to a nationality with a superabundance of freedom, and the large horses, firmly fixed in a vice, as it were, to a nationality doomed to be conscious every moment of their lives that they are hemmed in by hard, inflexible laws. Anyway, these large creatures feel at all times the "reins" of government.

And whilst I am talking about horses, let me just try to describe a little scene I witnessed. A struggling horse, and two energetic men; the horse plunging and kicking; the animal is being lifted into the air by two bands round the stomach; one of the men holds several yards of rope. Look carefully, and you will infer that the man is watching for an opportunity of coiling that rope round the leg of the animal. Now his point is gained; he has the leg in safe custody, and then hauls it any way he wishes, somewhat regardless of the direction nature intended that leg to move. He now hunts for instruments; surely, this is a case of horse-slaughter. Then comes a huge hammer. What is the fellow going to do? Why, he is only going to re-shoe the animal, to be sure!

And now to return to our midnight travelling. I was thinking of the two outer horses, and speculating how long this wonderfully-made harness could last, and

how soon the horses' legs would get entangled in the
odds and ends of ropes which were supposed to help in
keeping the horses together, when suddenly the second
horse disappeared! The driver gave a lurch forward;
the off-horse struggled; there was a bump and a thump
against the sledge, and then the other horse also
disappeared, and we came to a dead-lock. We were
both wide-awake in no time, and we heard and felt an
ominous knocking against the side; and on looking out
we found both horses entangled in the ropes and on the
ground, struggling frantically to get up.

The driver called "Nichivo" (It is nothing). But no
amount of "nichivoeing" prevented my feeling uneasy.
The soldier by this time had jumped off the box, and
there he stood abusing the horses, the driver, and the
road; then, finding that this failed to help matters
much, he began to spit at the horses. Then driver and
soldier stood still, looking helplessly on, not attempting
to do anything. I got my friend to translate a rather
peremptory order to both men; and this woke them up
to the fact that they must be doing something besides
abusing each other. By this time the poor horses were
getting tired of being jammed against the sledge and
tied up by the ropes, for their struggles became more
decided. The soldier quickly stood on one horse's
neck, and the driver set the harness free. The other
animal was treated in the same way; but the driver
was evidently too angry with it to drive it any more;

and so he just let it loose, and away it trotted, looking such an odd creature in the half snowlight, with the harness dragging all around it. The oddity of the scene made us enjoy a hearty laugh, notwithstanding the discomfort of the occasion. After a little more hard tugging and painful compulsion the three remaining horses were put, or rather tied, together, and away we started again.

But, somehow, our nerves were on the *qui vive* of expectancy, and sleep quite forsook our eye-lids. Something else was going to happen; of that we felt positive. Suddenly we heard a loud shouting, and, after a few minutes' speculation, we guessed that one of those continuous freight sledges, carrying goods to long distances, stood in our way. Our men shouted, but all to no purpose. We were going at a great speed, and of course expected a tremendous smash. In a few moments we were well on to the obstruction. A little horse, belonging to the other people, got terrified; it crossed our path, and we were sent flying into a deep ditch full of snow. It all happened like a flash of lightning. There in the ditch our horses stuck; not an inch would they budge, in spite of lashing, and tugging, and yelling. Like master, like horse. When you get into a difficulty, wait until somebody gets you out of it. There we were in a ditch at about one o'clock in the morning. We wanted to get out, but the soldier shouted, "Stay where you are, ladies." How-

ever, we thought differently, and managed to scramble
out, stepping into a snow-drift up to our knees; and we
stood shivering, like two forlorn, lost creatures, waiting
to be rescued. The men who had caused our trouble
went straight on without inquiring what had happened
—a custom not confined to this part of the world. I
stood in front of my friend, who was smaller than I,
trying to shelter her from the bitter wind. Whilst the
men flogged the horses and shouted at them we looked
on, wishing to help them in their task, but quite unable
to do so, clad in our cumbersome clothing. Then the driver
left us, and ran off to try and find the horse that had
deserted us. He was gone for half an hour, but his quest
was all in vain, for the sagacious animal had wandered
far away. Those blows that fell on the horses' backs
went to our hearts; but it was utterly useless for us to
interfere. Everything has an ending; and, at last, by
one mighty effort, horses and sledge were got out of the
ditch. We packed ourselves away into the sledge as
best we could, and once again started.

"It never rains but it pours." We galloped off and
soon found ourselves bumping over a ploughed field,
only scantily covered with snow; for the snow had
drifted into huge mounds. Round and round these
mounds we wandered, almost like traversing a maze,
only we failed to derive amusement from the diversion.
Then we came to a steep hill leading down to the river.
I woke up my friend just in time for her to catch a

glimpse of the same wretched horse, who had been the leader in the first mutiny, give a jerk and break the harness in three places, thus setting himself free. Then we went full tilt down on to the frozen river, the free horse keeping up with the others from sheer habit, and the harness dangling behind as usual. We expected another catastrophe every moment, and hardly knew whether to laugh or to cry. We chose the former alternative, and merrily awaited events. On reaching the river, the driver got down, tied up the broken harness, abused the horses, and then tore away again.

Now we thought we should be safe; but, alas! we were not yet "out of the wood." The driver had worked himself into a towering rage, and now dashed on, heedless of everything. As we raced through a village, the middle horse stumbled and fell, and we found ourselves firmly wedged in a drift. Another war of words arose between soldier and driver. "They are not horses, but demons!" roared the soldier to the youth, as blow after blow fell on the jaded horses' backs. We got out of the muddle after the usual struggle and outburst of high words. Another short spin, and we arrived at the post-station at two o'clock in the morning.

The hard, dirty floor we hailed with delight, and slept heavily for five hours. At some of the post-stations other travellers may be found, of various ages and of both sexes, and they all have to find places on the one floor for the night. Sometimes we were disturbed in the midst of a peaceful slumber by the crying of an infant; but, as a rule, we were too ready for sleep to pay any attention to disturbances of any kind. Now and then a clean post-station may be met with; but, generally speaking, they are places to be avoided. As to the state of the atmosphere in the morning, after a number of people, enveloped in dirty sheepskins, have been enjoying repose, and the room without a chink of ventilation, I leave to the reader's imagination.

We arrived at Tobolsk about midnight the following day. Having been previously told that the Governor had kindly engaged a room for us at the hotel, we naturally expected that something nice was in store. Passing the little wooden houses, we saw, not far off, a large brick building. "Oh, that will do," we thought; "just the thing!"

It was rather disappointing to be told that this was the Governor's house. However, we were confident that the hotel would suddenly loom from round some corner, and were still eagerly expectant. We were then driven into a yard, not of the cleanest, and we wondered what our man meant by calling at such a place, and thought that there must surely be some mistake. Adjacent to the yard was a large, tumble-down, wooden house. That was the hotel! Grieving over baffled hopes, we mounted a flight of stairs and entered a room, the air of which was stiflingly hot.

A hot room is always a Russian's welcome to a guest, and, of course, the higher the temperature of the room the warmer the feelings of the host. This hotel-keeper must have overflowed with cordial sentiments. The double windows were cemented all round, in order to destroy the remotest chance of fresh air entering. The room contained two bedsteads and one mattress. (This was one out of many hotels where visitors were expected to bring their own sheets.) The walls were not clean; it would be unbecoming, with such a warm reception, to speak more definitely on that point. We saw plainly enough that we should have to sleep on the floor, after all. But the room grew hotter and hotter, although the door had been open for a considerable time; and we began to feel ill. I contemplated adopting a swift and drastic method of letting in a breath of air, but feared that the noise of falling glass might create a commotion in the house, and, perhaps, through the whole town. Then I discovered at one of the windows that the glass had at some time or another been broken, and then plastered over with paper. So I carefully removed the fragments, put my hand through the opening, and pushed hard through the second window, and, lo, the deed was done! Then we went to sleep on the floor.

We were compensated for the inconveniences suffered at this hotel, by the pleasant surprise the next day on visiting the prison. We found there admirable arrangements in every way. As regards cleanliness and sanitary precautions nothing could be better. Each cell contained but a few prisoners, and the various sections of religionists were kept apart in separate quarters. Instead of the *nares* (sloping boards), for sleeping upon, proper beds were provided with mattresses, and were slung up against the wall in the daytime. The hospital also was very clean, and by no means overcrowded. As we walked through one of the wards, a prisoner gave my friend a letter, which a police official in a few moments took out of her hands and read.

"You don't thrash these fellows enough," said he, in an undertone, to another official standing at the door.

My friend, overhearing what the officer said, translated it to me, and I at once appealed to him on the prisoner's behalf. After much pleading he promised to forgive the offence, and not to thrash the culprit.

There is a clean and inviting church attached to the prison, and a pretty little museum in the town. One of my chief objects in coming to Tobolsk was to see the governor about the polluted river. He invited us to lunch with him, and I there laid before him the pitiable case of these poor villagers. He took a warm interest in the matter and promised to investigate it himself.

At every village station where we stopped, as we proceeded on our journey, numbers of peasants used to assemble, attracted by the red cross on the sledge, which I had been advised to have painted there, as an indication of my connection with the Russian Red Cross Society. As soon as they knew that I was a sister of charity, they used to press into the little room where we were having our tea, bringing their sick and suffering for help. As much as I could I ministered to their bodies, whilst my friend spoke to them of the great Physician. They were eagerly attentive, seeming, with both ears and eyes, to drink in every word, and a bright smile lit up their countenances as we gave them the little Testaments and Gospels which we had brought with us. The thought came to me that perhaps no woman-missionary had passed this way. I knew I was the least worthy to do any work for the Master; but as I looked at the eager faces around me, I asked Him to use me in bringing to the people I came across the glad tidings of great joy.

At the next station my friend found that the driver could read, so we at once gave him a Gospel. Then two other men came up and asked for copies. One was able to read, and the other, an old white-haired man, intended to take the Gospel to his little grandson who would read it to him. As I looked at these men, with their hats off, begging for the Word of Life and Peace, I asked God to bless it to them, and knew that in His own time it would bear fruit. I pictured the old man tottering home, and, in the evening, sitting by the dim light of a tallow candle, earnestly listening to the little child, who, with his finger on the page, was slowly spelling one sentence after the other. Thus the Lord was, I believed, answering my prayer. When the people gathered round us at the villages, we generally had a good opportunity of giving away Testaments and speaking to them of Christ. It was often a motley group: grey-haired men and women, bowed with age; young people, looking on with curious, inquiring looks; children in their quaint frocks and tunics—all trying to catch a glimpse of our faces.

As we went on, the road became worse and worse, and my friend fell ill from sheer fatigue and want of proper food. We were obliged to stop at Tukalinsk, where we arrived thoroughly exhausted. Here we became the objects of some thoughtfulness, for the post-station being too dirty for habitation, orders had been given to take us to a well-to-do peasant's house. The soldiers led us up the steps, and we were put into quite a comfortable room, like one in an English farm-house. We sat down, and were too ill to speak or to undress. After taking some hot coffee we slept like logs all night, my friend on the sofa and I on the floor, an arrangement upon which I firmly insisted, because she was younger than I.

We rested till the afternoon of the following day, and then hired a sledge to take us round the town—a queer little place, with the houses all tumbled together, built of solid trunks of trees. The greater part of the population consisted of convicts. We were out about half an hour; but as the man took us past the church four times, I have a shrewd suspicion that he took us round and round the same places.

In the evening we had quite a *levée*. The head of the village, or mayor, a portly person in full dress, with chain, sword, braided jacket, and white kid gloves, and four doctors, came to see us. They sat and talked for nearly four hours, all the men smoking cigarettes. The mayor led the conversation, and, long before the visitors left, our throats and heads ached from the talk, and the smoke, and the heat. It was arranged that we should see the prisoners next morning, and that the five gentlemen would come and escort us. One of them, a veterinary surgeon, presented me with a beautiful model of a church, made by two convicts with an old knife in a dark cell. The next morning, on setting off to the prisons, a severe *bourran*, or snow-storm, was raging, and the little Siberian horses were very reluctant to take the road.

We found in Tukalinsk, besides the regular convicts within the prison walls, a great number of those who had served their time, and were free, but unable to get employment, and, perhaps, unwilling. They led a vagrant life, begging from door to door. The residents of the little town had taken compassion, and had built a little two-roomed house as a night-refuge, where they huddled together. Many of the latter miserable fellows

came round us begging, with hardly any clothes to cover
them, some shoeless, and all hungry. The scene they
presented was indeed a piteous one. On reaching the
prison we could see nothing but tall wooden palings
and the summit of the church. Once inside we found a
terrible state of things, which contrasted forcibly with
the splendid prison we had seen in Tobolsk. It was all
the more striking as it was in the same government,
and under the same governor; but I was told that a
new prison was shortly to be built. The place was
built to hold seventy; but the usual number of
prisoners is two hundred. The floors were rotten from
damp, and the walls bulged from the same cause.
There was no ventilation, and all sanitary matters were
wofully neglected. No English woman had ever
visited this place, and we therefore prized the privilege
of being able to speak to the poor fellows. We had
taken some tea and sugar, which we distributed, and
then spoke of Christ, giving away Testaments, which
were eagerly accepted.

Perhaps some friends might think that this trifling
attention to the physical needs of prisoners was super-
fluous, and that I ought to have been contented with
spiritual ministration. But I asked myself, I hope not
presumptuously, what Christ would have done? And
I felt that He would first attend in some degree to the
material wants of such outcasts, before offering the
Bread of Life. Then, too, I knew that the convicts

love their tea, and, when once they were sent off to Siberia, tea was seldom provided for them, and being permitted to give this trifling luxury, I tried to reach their hearts by first attending to their bodies.

I told them to look out for me on the road, when they were moving from place to place, that they could always identify me by the red cross on the sledge, and that I should be always ready to help them as far as I could. Running short of tea and sugar, we had to come the next day with more, and again tried to turn the men's thoughts to the love and sympathy of Christ, and to the hope beyond their present miseries. Now and then some hard face would suddenly light up, as if that hope had already given a moment of joy. Poor fellows! I have nothing to do with their crimes, and can offer no criticism on prison administration in Russia; but I firmly believe that, when it becomes practicable to carry out measures of improvement, no time will be lost in accomplishing that desirable end.

The head policeman spoke very kindly to these men; they were not frightened and scared, as is generally the case on the approach of their jailer.

Later in the day, as we were going out, a wretchedly-clad convict, but a very fine-looking fellow, came up and put an envelope into my hand. He shivered with cold, and looked as if all hope was crushed for ever. I promised to give him what assistance I could, telling him that I intended visiting the night-refuge the next morning, and would no doubt see him there.

The following is the translation of the letter:—

"Tukalinsk, Siberia, March 10th, 1891.

"YOUR HIGHNESS,

"Having heard of your charitable visits to the poor and oppressed people, we unfortunate convicts, living in the night-refuge house which is kept up by the inhabitants of the town of Tukalinsk, dare to appeal to your Highness to give any kind of help to people who have no possibility of earning anything, and who are in a constant struggle for daily life."

We visited the vagabond house, or night-refuge house, and found the men packed like herrings. It was as much as we could do to pass down sideways, I giving tea and sugar and the little Gospels, and my friend speaking of the Word of Life.

CHAPTER IV.

CLANKING CHAINS.

Home comforts at Omsk—An additional escort provided—Omsk
prison and hospital—Free dinners for the poor—Deserted!—
Meeting a gang of prisoners on the road—Scene in an *étape*—
A great work for Russian ladies—Improvements in prison
administration—Tomsk and its prisons—Haunted dreams—
Dangers of crossing thawing rivers.

OUR journey from Tukalinsk to Omsk was accomplished
without any particular mishap, but with the usual discomforts. At the last post-station, before reaching the
latter place, a soldier was waiting to tell us that the
Governor of Omsk, General Sannikoff, had prepared
rooms for our reception in his own house. This was
cheerful news, for we were in no way reluctant to renew
our acquaintance with feather beds and the comforts of
the family circle. It was especially welcome, because
both my companion and myself would have been
considered, under ordinary circumstances, fit objects for
a doctor's attention. And, perhaps, it was really about
time that we took a little physic.

We received a most kind and warm welcome at the
Governor's house, and were treated throughout our stay

of about a fortnight as members of the family. This long visit was owing chiefly to my ill-health ; and I am greatly indebted to the nursing, attention, and medical aid which I received in the Governor's home.

Much to my regret, it was found absolutely necessary that my friend Miss Field should return home, on account of her continued bad health. She had been interpreter, as well as faithful companion and helper throughout the journey, and I dreaded to think of the difficulties I should have to encounter without her presence.

Our prayers for guidance and help were not in vain. Before reaching Omsk we had been troubled with a tipsy driver. Somehow or other the General-Governor had heard of the matter ; and it was his opinion that someone more efficient than the common soldier was needed to protect us. So he telegraphed a request to the Governor of Tomsk, who at once sent a special official, one of his attachés. This gentleman arrived at Omsk in four days, thus swiftly traversing a distance of about 800 miles. He could speak French and a little English, and, being also thoroughly well versed in his own language, all fears of future emergencies disappeared. So my dear friend left me, intending to interest sympathisers at home in the work to which I was committed.

The prison at Omsk was in excellent condition. The Governor, out of a good heart, showed great kindness to the inmates, allowing them to work, to sell their goods, and to keep the proceeds for themselves. He often bought articles of their production for his own use, and sought to render their sad lives bearable and bright. He assembled the prisoners in the dining-hall, where we gave them small packets of tea and sugar, and spoke of Christ. The Governor acted as interpreter, and added to what I said.

The Military Hospital is a fine establishment, containing about three hundred soldiers, who are all well cared for. We gave a Gospel to each of the soldiers, who showed gratifying appreciation of this little effort to serve them.

There is a hall in the town where free dinners are provided for the poor, so that, even in these outlying parts of the Empire, the spirit of practical philanthropy is happily illustrated. It was a gratifying sight to see about a hundred of the poorer inhabitants, of all ages and of both sexes, sitting down to an ample meal of wholesome food ; and my thoughts turned for a moment to the same kind of thing going on in England to minister to the wants of the unfortunate people of the slums. After the meal I spoke of God's love, and gave away Testaments, and felt that, on the whole, this was the most pleasing scene I had witnessed since leaving Moscow. The schools were also visited, and Testaments distributed amongst the children.

On leaving Omsk I had the misfortune, before many

miles had been covered, to be at the mercy of another tipsy driver. The harness-gear of the middle horse broke with a sharp crack; there was a great deal of shouting and then perfect stillness, which lulled me to sleep. I awoke to find myself with the tipsy driver curled up asleep on the box, the two horses standing with no one to look after them. The stillness was dreadful; I was utterly helpless, and the blinding snow dashed in my face. Presently I was startled by seeing a strange man, also tipsy, standing at my side. He proved to be a Yemstchick, or driver of a freight sledge that was passing by. From his maudlin utterances I gathered that the soldier had taken the third horse to some village for new harness, and the official, being some good way in advance in his sledge, had not noticed this mishap.

It was certainly not a pleasant position for a helpless woman to be in; but I tried not to think of danger. I knew, however, that the mistaken idea had got abroad that I was rich; and so, "putting two and two together," the suspicion arose that desperate robbers, lurking in the forest, would suddenly pounce upon me. At such times real and imaginary dangers intermix. I thought that my men deserting me was only part of a conspiracy, and my mind dwelt on the fact that I was in the land of convicts, 40,000 of them being sent hither every year. The hour of suspense seemed six hours; but at last the soldier returned with the horse, with new harness. It was put in his place, and we started off again.

We went on about fifteen miles, and by that time the moon had risen. Presently the horses shied; and, on looking out, I saw a poor dead horse, which some dogs were quarrelling over. The blood-stained snow, and the animal's flesh torn off, sent a shudder through me. I saw a similar horrible sight over and over again in the course of my travels, but one reference to such a subject is quite sufficient. When a horse in these Siberian deserts and forests becomes exhausted and can go no further, it is unharnessed and left to its fate. Siberian drivers say that, if such an over-worked horse recovers, he will find his way home in due time, but if not—well, they don't trouble about the matter. Sometimes an over-worked horse is left standing in the desert, but in too weak a condition to resist the attacks of the savage dogs. What a fate for the poor faithful creatures!

On reaching Kainsk we heard that a party of prisoners were in the neighbourhood, on their way from the frontier. A strong *bourran* (snowstorm) was blowing; and I could imagine the poor people struggling through it. So I longed to overtake them, to give them the bits of tea and sugar, in order that they might have something to warm themselves with at the next post-station.

I inquired at each post-station, but could learn

nothing at first. I was groaning under the almost
intolerable pain caused by the constant lurching of the
sledge. I asked at another station for the *arriastanty*
(prisoners), but was promptly told that there were none.
Even my old soldier was getting irritable from my
pertinacity. At last I found out that there were
prisoners in some cells who were to start the next
morning, and I set off to visit them. "It was too late,"
I was told; "they were being locked up for the night;"
but, as the cold wind pierced me, I knew what comfort
a little tea would be to them before they started. I
persevered, and succeeded in making my way to the
place.

The entrance to the two large cells was quite dark.
Two soldiers stood on guard, as usual, with guns and
bayonets ready. It was so dark inside that I could
only hear the rattle of the chains as the officers called
out "Attention!" But I felt there were human beings
all around me, and, indeed, there were ninety of them
crammed into this hole, with not the slightest ventilation. One prisoner led the way, holding a small piece
of candle. The men were lying down the centre, and
on each side, on boards raised a few feet from the floor,
and also under these boards, packed so closely that
they had hardly room to breathe. They stared at me,
half dazed at seeing a woman, alone, amongst them.
They put out their hands for the Gospels; but I
wondered they did not kill me in their desperation, and

how easily they could have done it! Instead of killing
me, they blessed my hands for the little gifts. I went
along sideways, sometimes half stumbling over those
who were lying down in the centre, and who had not
heard me coming, and so bringing a look of terror to
their faces. There was one little hump-backed fellow
who looked quite ghastly, and, near him, I stumbled
against a man on the floor, only saving myself from
falling by catching hold of two other prisoners. How
tenderly these men helped me! Their rough hands
were as gentle as any woman's. At the end of about
three-quarters of an hour I had to leave, for a faintness
came over me from the foul air; but, had I fainted, I
should have been as safe amongst those ninety convicts
as in my own home in England. On saying "Good
night" I peered into the darkness towards the men
beyond in the next cell, and heard the clanking of their
chains, and the groans of those who were ill from fatigue;
but even their thanks rose in one shout, from end to end,
as I went out; and the door was shut and padlocked
on those ninety men, lost to their country and to every
joy and every comfort of life. May God have mercy!
May He bless those little Gospels, and let them be the
means of making those sin-laden people look up to
One who is able to save, even them, to the uttermost!

I went to rest; but could rest come to me, with that
awful picture in my eyes, and those groans and the
rattle of the chains ringing in my ears? At five the

next morning I started on my way. Travelling from place to place, one gets accustomed to meeting the gangs of weary men and women on their way from the capital and large towns. First of all, a black mass is discovered in the distance; then, on getting a little nearer, the soldiers' bayonets glitter in the sunlight; nearer still, you can hear the dismal clank of the chains, and soon the gang is close at hand. In order to ensure discipline, it is found necessary to shoot any prisoner who attempts to regain his liberty. An open sledge usually accompanies the party for anyone who falls ill on the way.

On meeting such a company, I usually ordered the driver to stop, and then prepared to go amongst the convicts. I never could go to them clad in furs from head to foot, with my morsels of tea and sugar, when they were only scantily clothed, and every blast of wind pierced through and through them. My furs would almost have burnt me had I gone to the poor creatures thus clad. So I took off some of them; then, stuffing the large pockets of my ulster with tea and sugar, and with two large bags strapped over my shoulders, and getting a soldier to carry two or three baskets, I went into the midst of the gang. To see the grateful looks of those men, as I put one of the packets of tea and sugar and a Testament into their hands, was worth all the trials I had suffered, and all that were to come. As my bare hands became numbed from exposure to the cold, and the icy wind went through me, I realised, in some trifling measure, the same physical suffering which they were enduring. I gave a double quantity of tea and sugar to the women, who sometimes were nursing their babies. I have often seen children with these parties, but open sledges were generally provided for them. Some of the women were convicts, and others were accompanying their husbands, from their own choice, into banishment, to be supported at Government expense, taking their children with them. It is utterly impossible to describe one's feelings when witnessing such scenes as these; but the tender-hearted and all lovers of humanity will understand what I experienced. After wishing the people " Good-bye," and creeping into my sledge, a sense of misery would come over me, and, at the same time, a sense of gratitude to God for allowing me to give them even " a drop of cold water " in His name.

How unworthy I felt to do this work ! but I prayed God to make me less unworthy. It is a mission that only the noblest, bravest, and purest in the land should do. And I am so faulty ! Oh, dear Russian ladies, here is work for you ! It is, indeed, woman's work. Oh ! let the condition of these poor creatures, guilty though they may be, bring you into this field, " white unto the harvest."

There are many in St. Petersburg and Russia who are devoting their whole lives to the bettering of the

prisons in Siberia and elsewhere; and none but those
who have travelled through it can understand the
immense improvements that have been instituted; and
I am only mentioning these various prisons and scenes
as contrasts, in order to show the difference where
improvements have been introduced, and where they
have not. My work was to get to the lepers; and it
was only through the courtesy of certain people that
I was allowed to visit the prisons and *étapes.* Some of
them are undeniably terrible; but every year vast improvements are carried out; and I dare say that, by
now, many of the sad scenes I witnessed are a thing of
the past. In many places along the road I found earnest
workers amongst the prisoners, and priests who were
devoting their lives to them; and this desire to minister
to their needs is manifested all through Siberia. The
still far-off lepers were not forgotten; but, I could not
hasten on, and refrain from these small efforts amongst
the convicts. Then, too, a feeling was uppermost that
I was doing this work on my journey in obedience to
the voice of God. Little did I think, when leaving
Moscow, that such a work would be granted to me,
and such opportunities given for ministering, even in a
small degree, to the criminals of Russia.

On arriving at Tomsk, in April, I was too ill to visit
the prisons immediately, and had to wait, trying to get
strength, for two days. I went to the hospital first,
and then to the prisons, where I gave food comforts

and Testaments to over 2000 prisoners. To describe in detail all I saw would do no good, especially as many of the sad sights I witnessed are a thing of the past. Owing to the earnest representations of the Governor, the Government has granted a large sum of money for new prisons and hospitals.

Can it be wondered at that, when I retired to rest at night, after visiting day by day these scenes, my dreams were haunted by desperate convicts, threatening murderers, awful-looking women, poor starving children, and ever-clanging chains? And the faces of those exiles haunt me still.

The day before leaving Tomsk, the police-master of Krasnoyarsk very kindly came to warn me against the dangerous condition of the rivers and roads. His own sledge in travelling to Tomsk had gone through the ice, and he had barely escaped drowning. The following day he accompanied me to Krasnoyarsk. We had to cross in a heavy tarantass, a vehicle generally used in place of a sledge when the breaking-up season has fairly commenced. I shall have something to say later on about this nerve-shaking and bone-trying contrivance.

On reaching the river it was quite evident that there was danger ahead, for the police-master alighted from his carriage, and sent on a man to ascertain the condition of the ice. At this time of the year all the rivers become very dangerous. The ice begins to

crack and to melt; then it freezes slightly again, so
that it is difficult to make sure whether, on leaving one
side, you will ever arrive at the other. Sometimes
straw is laid on the partly-melted ice so as to bind the
cracked ice with the next frost. The man returned
with his report; and then his courteous master offered
me a seat in his light carriage to take me across, which
was a clear intimation that if we had ventured on the
ice in a heavy tarantass, we should have gone under,
horses and all. Many lives are lost in the course of a
year on these treacherous rivers. As we drove in the
carriage, premonitory cracks were heard below, which
created a little uneasiness. On landing safely we
found, in a few minutes, that there was an old, shaky
bridge to cross, which, we were told, was more unsafe
than the river, and which was studiously avoided.
However, the bridge must be crossed, and we tried our
best not to think about danger. The crazy thing shook
a great deal, but we got over without an accident, thank
God!

The dangers one has to face in crossing the thawing rivers were again forcibly impressed upon me near
Krasnoyarsk. We had to cross the Yenessei, one of
many broad rivers whose acquaintance I had made in
the course of my journey. This river, like others, was
very broad, containing an immense volume of water.
On beginning to cross, the opposite side could hardly be
discerned. The feelings of a nervous woman may well

be imagined as we ventured on to the moist, cracked surface. Straw was laid, as usual, but it seemed to be of little service. Sometimes, when a feeling of dizziness came on, I shut my eyes; but I knew I was in God's hands, and felt sure that no accident would happen, and that He would allow me to reach my final destination amongst the lepers. When the other side was safely reached, my feelings of relief and gratitude may well be imagined.

CHAPTER V.

TARANTASS TRAVELLING.

Krasnoyarsk, and its institutions—Improvements in the Russian prison system—Character of true Siberian—Buying a tarantass — How to "mount" a tarantass — Tarantass "rheumatism," its diagnosis and development—Kansk and its prison—Crossing a ferry, and arrival at Irkutsk.

KRASNOYARSK, about five hundred miles from Tomsk, is a pretty place. The inhabitants call it "lovely," and so it is, when you drive out of the town into the suburbs. The town is pretty and attractive in many ways. The prison is in admirable condition, well managed, with good ventilation, and proper sanitary provisions. I wish again to draw particular attention to the fact, now that Krasnoyarsk prison is mentioned, that improvements are going on, although slowly, in the Russian prison system, and, before many years elapse, we shall probably see reforms carried out universally, similar to those at Krasnoyarsk, Omsk, and other large centres.

Improvements are also contemplated with respect to the *étapes*. In about six years, when various railway projects have been realised. many of the present abuses will be at an end, and, amongst them, the *étapes*. But, in the meantime, let not Christian workers in Russia withhold active help in meeting the wants of the prisoners. Even when prisons are made more wholesome and healthy, the need will still exist for Christian and philanthropic effort, similar to that carried on in so many parts of the world.

Besides the excellent prison there is a beautiful little hospital at Krasnoyarsk, supported by some of the inhabitants. All the appliances of the latest scientific discoveries, as well as the best systems of nursing, are here in operation. Another institution in this town is the Home for Orphans, established by a benevolent lady, and kept in perfect condition. The impression conveyed during my stay in the place was of a very delightful nature. I felt that all the people were striving to help one another, and were thus bound together by a cordial and sympathetic relationship. They were, in fact, specimens of true Siberians, reminding me very much of British Colonials—frank, honest, upright, truthful and loyal. They will give a welcome to every stranger, and help all in need. They have a great love for the Czar, but a natural antipathy to officials, who put a wrong construction upon Imperial orders, and carry out such orders in accordance with their own private interpretations, rather than in harmony with the Emperor's wishes. But neither this, nor anything else, shakes their allegiance and devotion to their Czar.

I had to buy a tarantass before leaving, and created quite a stir by my efforts to come out on the right side of a bargain. Three specimens of this vehicle were brought for me to see, all rubbishing affairs. For one of them I was asked the modest sum of fifty roubles. I packed off men and vehicles, energetically shaking my head, and saying " No." In half an hour there were other arrivals, worse than the first ; and the price demanded was seventy roubles each. To end matters, I said I should take a tarantass belonging to the Governor. By this time a crowd of villagers had collected to see a foreigner do business. There was a great deal of whispering and talking, and then, when the owners of different vehicles began quarrelling and fighting, the hubbub was immense. To see these men fight would have brought a look of contempt on the faces of English fighters. There were no double fists ; it was simply an amiable encounter to see which could lay the other on the ground first. I thought whether it was possible to carry on wars after the same pattern, that is, without the shedding of blood and the infliction of pain. After a lot more chattering, a messenger was sent to me to say I might have a sound and safe tarantass for thirty roubles. I accepted the offer, and also gained valuable experience in doing business.

Then began the packing of my tarantass, which was no trivial affair. It must be packed carefully, otherwise the ordinary miseries of travelling in such a thing would be considerably intensified. Now, this vehicle, which was never designed for comfort, is innocent of a single spring. It runs on wheels, and stands a long way from the ground, making it awkward for a woman to get in without assistance. The roads at this time of the year are in a terrible condition; a ploughed field, containing a good many deep ruts, is the nearest description I can give of them. When a thaw commences the soft, pulpy state of affairs begins; then there comes a slight frost and a thin layer of ice, frequently misleading the traveller. When he thinks he is going to glide along in tolerable ease, he suddenly bumps down through the ice into a great hole of sticky, pulpy mud, or if there has been a very severe frost during the night, all the roads are turned into solid blocks of frozen mud. I know the roads are in excellent condition in some seasons of the year; but it was not my good fortune to travel at such propitious times.

Now, when you are once in a tarantass, loaded in the "hold" with all sorts of packages, upon which you lie, you have to make up your mind before starting that, during a journey of one thousand miles or so, you will be brave, patient, and resigned. At the very first move of the vehicle you will probably find yourself thrown on to its edge, with your poor feet dashed against the front part, which consists of sharp wood. Then, after scrambling back into position, the thing lurches, and you feel as if you were trying in vain to keep up with it ; but, after an hour, you give up all effort, and leave your body to do just what is required. By that time, you have realised in what way the spirit of resignation must be testified. But the body itself begins to complain after the lapse of another hour or two ; and that is just where the " pinch " is, for you cannot, unfortunately, infuse the spirit of resignation into your body.

Your limbs ache, your muscles ache, your head aches, and, worst of all, your inside aches terribly. " Tarantass rheumatism," internal and external, chronic, or, rather, perpetual, is the complaint from which you will have to suffer during that thousand miles. At the end of the first day you would like a feather bed for about a week ; but, in case there is no hotel accommodation on the route as the day declines, why, then, you must go on all night in your conveyance. Of course, you will sleep, and awake nice and fresh at breakfast time. But at sunset, and probably before that hour, you will hanker after that feather bed again, with the addition of a little kind nursing and skilful medical attention. Possibly you may pull up at an hotel the next night ; but, by that time, your body declines to take any active exercise in a perpendicular position, and so you stay where you are. In the course of the next twenty-four hours, a faint, vapid sort of feeling creeps over you, which may be vulgarly termed " don't care." A little farther, and, somehow, you don't remember the consecutive order of

events in your past life, particularly the latter portion
of it. The next day you become strangely oblivious to
wind and weather, and everything. And now, several
hundred miles or so being accomplished, and having
been carried to your quarters, in a more oblivious state
than ever, you have no wish save just one—and that is,
for a month's rest and sleep.

On reaching Kansk, I visited the prison, which is a
large one. I found, in front of it, the usual number of
women, selling bread and soup to the prisoners; and I
gladly bought all they had, and so went in, quite rich
in gifts. Every tiny window was crowded with numerous
heads, all trying to have a peep at me. I found 186
men, all in chains. On seeing us bringing the food a
perfect babel of voices greeted us; and even the presence
of the officers did not quiet them, two men taking
my hand, and smoothing it with theirs, whilst tears
rolled down their cheeks, and down mine, too. They
all crowded as close as they could to get near me, and
their faces brightened, often with a smile, as I spoke
two or three sentences in half-broken Russian. All the
way down the ranks their continuous thanking showed
how really grateful they were for even the small help
we brought them. But it is not so much the little help
as *the desire to help them* that they realise. In one cell
were twenty murderers; they were placed here, owing
to no separate cells being empty. I went amongst
them, at my own request, with only a man to carry the

provisions and Testaments, in the hope that God would bless the desire to speak to them, and lead them to read His Word. On distributing tea and sugar and the little books, their angry, hardened, and almost de-humanised faces slowly softened. On leaving, one of the men, with ready politeness, showed me out of the cell, as it was too dark to see my way.

And now, on setting off from Kansk, I looked forward with anticipation, not unmixed with fear, to my visit to Irkutsk. It was here I expected to collect a number of particulars about the lepers of Yakutsk, and to be assisted in various ways in the prosecution of the objects I had in view. I arrived at Irkutsk in a piti-able condition, which need not be described in any detailed form, for, after what has been said about tarantass riding in the breaking-up season, my plight may easily be imagined. However, I was not too ill to notice for a moment the picturesque aspect of the town as we approached it. Its multitude of churches, and the dainty way in which they seem to be built and decorated; its broad, beautiful river, its undulating hills—all gave one the idea of civilisation, and I seemed to breathe freely again after the desolation and discom-fort of the road. We had to cross a ferry, and the tarantass, with all its contents, myself included, was wheeled on to the boat, which was very small, and looked unsafe. The boat was partly paddled and partly hauled across by a rope. The current was strong and I wanted to get out of the tarantass, so that I might have a chance of being rescued in case we were capsized. Such an accident happened once when the archbishop and all his clergy were crossing. However, we landed safely; and glad enough I was to get into the hotel. For two days I could scarcely walk; my body ached and smarted as if it had been beaten. As I thanked God with all my heart that He had brought me safely thus far, I felt that nothing in the world would induce me to undertake the journey again, except spreading, in a humble way, the Gospel of Christ and helping the lepers.

CHAPTER VI.

NEARING THE LEPERS.

Committee formed at Irkutsk—My reception at the meeting, and
the results of the deliberations—Official documents showing
the position of the lepers in the Viluisk Circuit since 1827—
Sixty-four years' pleading—Miseries of the Yakutsk lepers—
The leper-outcast's doom—Departure for Yakutsk—Journey
up the Lena—Chasing the Governor's steamer—Arrival in
Yakutsk.

AFTER resting two days in Irkutsk I called upon the
General-Governor, who received me with great kindness. He corroborated all I had heard about the state
of the Yakutsk lepers, and, whilst adding to my information, was quite eager in offering his services to help
them. I suggested the formation of a committee of
influential people in Irkutsk, who could arouse the
sympathy and obtain the help of the merchants of the
town on behalf of their poor lost brethren in the north.
We discussed the many difficulties which surrounded
the subject, especially the difficulty of evoking sympathy for people whose woeful condition was almost
unknown.

His Excellency graciously consented to form a committee, and at length decided that it should consist of

the following persons: the Governor-General, His Grace the Archbishop of Irkutsk, His Grace the Archbishop of Kirensk, the cathedral priest Vinogradoff, His Excellency the State Councillor Sievers, the Inspector of Medicine, the Aide-de-camp of the Commander of troops, Captain Lvoff, the Mayor, and myself.

The first meeting was appointed for May 1st (13th), my birthday, and one of the happiest days of my life, for my plans were now to receive official recognition and aid.

At eleven o'clock the captain came to me and read over the order of proceedings in French. Then we drove to the palace of the Archbishop, and as the carriage stopped at the gates, my heart gave many a flutter of anticipation and hope, as well as of nervous, unaccountable dread.

We walked up the steps into the hall, where I put on my cap, and then we went into the large reception hall. In five minutes His Excellency the General-Governor, in full uniform, came in, followed by the Mayor, Councillor Sievers, and the Inspector of Medicine. After a brief interval the large doors were thrown open, and His Grace the Archbishop entered in full canonicals and orders. The Governor went up to him first, and received his blessing, kissing his cheeks and his mouth. A few minutes after the Archbishop of Kirensk arrived, and we all went into the drawing-room, furnished with dark and light yellow draperies which stood out in striking contrast to the robes of the Archbishop, and the dresses of the other members. What a strange meeting it was! As I knew only a few words of Russian, the proceedings were translated to me by Captain Lvoff. I was treated with the utmost kindness and courtesy by all present, each trying to surpass the other in politeness and kind attentions. They promised to carry out every suggestion, and bound themselves to help in every way in their power. It was amusing to see the shy manner in which they glanced at me every now and then. Really, the tables seemed to be turned, and my nervousness and alarm seemed to be transferred to them. We had glasses of tea, or, rather, they, for I was provided with a special cup, which appeared lost among the glasses, just as I looked among these great people. We talked for two hours and then went into the hall. I had begged that our photographs might be taken later on, as a remembrance of this special meeting on behalf of the lepers, hoping it was the beginning of real and continuous help for them. So we were all taken in a group; and, after a few words of farewell, we separated.

The following extract from the minutes of the meeting was afterwards sent on to me by Captain Lvoff.

" The said members decided as follows :—

" 1. To take no steps until Miss Marsden personally inspects the position of the lepers of the Viluisk Circuit.

and gets acquainted with the exact number of lepers. For this last purpose she will have to address a set of medical questions to them. The committee will only give its decision when Miss Marsden has presented her report and opinion as to the best way of alleviating the position of the lepers.

" 2. The Archbishop expressed his intention to write a letter to the Bishop of Yakutsk and Viluisk, commending Miss Marsden to his care and help.

" 3. It was decided to send a telegram to the Medical Department, asking them to send a copy of Dr. Krasnoff's report about leprosy in the Viluisk Circuit in 1865.

" The minutes of the above decisions were written down for Miss Marsden by the Secretary, Captain Lvoff, Aide-de-camp to the Governor.

" Irkutsk, May 27th, 1891."

During the next day or two I made arrangements for setting off to Yakutsk; but, before giving an account of that journey, it is desirable to supply the reader, at this stage, with a few details I had received respecting the lepers in the above district. The General-Governor furnished me with an official statement, of which the following is a translation by Captain Lvoff, showing the position of the lepers during the last sixty-four years. I trust the reader will give these documents his careful attention, as well as every other document

quoted in this book. They fully bear out every detail
I have mentioned and shall mention. With all the
contradictions and opposite statements about Siberia at
the present moment, it is necessary to have Russian
official documents as confirmatory evidence of all that
is stated.

Document 1.

"In 1827 the Viluisk doctor first gave information
that among the Yakuts of the Viluisk Circuit had
appeared an incurable disease, called leprosy. Dr.
Krusé confirmed this report, saying that this disease
had been devastating the land for some time past.
With regard to hospitals, there was only one miserable
yourta, which held five lepers at that time, and seven
other patients suffering from other diseases, and all the
patients were under one roof. Dr. Uklonsky, seeing
the frightful condition of this yourta, addressed a
petition to the Committee of Hospitals and Medical
Institutions in Siberia, asking them to build a small
hospital in Viluisk, if only for fifteen patients, and
asking the Committee to buy, for that purpose, his
own house, costing 500 roubles. This house was bought
in 1834. In 1835 the Yakutsk Government informed
the General-Governor that the house that had been
bought was not fit for a hospital, that it was old
and badly built, and that it was impossible to place
patients in it.

"In this state affairs dragged on till 1839. In 1840

the Head Medical Inspector was himself a witness of the sufferings endured by the lepers in this yourta, and he was convinced that it was absolutely necessary to build a hospital for twenty-five patients.   The engineers informed the General-Governor that, for building a hospital, the sum of 12,857 roubles would be necessary. In 1843 the Governor of Yakutsk informed the General-Governor that there was a house to be sold in Viluisk for 1200 roubles, and that, by purchasing this house, an economy of more than 10,000 roubles would be effected.   But in 1845 the Governor wrote to the General-Governor that this house was also in a bad condition, and that they must decide to erect a new building.   In 1846 the General-Governor informed the Minister of the Interior that a hospital in Viluisk was absolutely necessary, and that it must be built at the expense of the Government, as the Siberian Committee of Hospitals could not incur the expense of the said building, in view of the insufficiency of present funds. In 1852 the Minister of the Interior informed the General-Governor that the condition of the State finances would not permit of the before-mentioned expense, and that the Committee must find the necessary means to build a hospital.   In 1855 the Governor of Yakutsk informed the General-Governor that there was a capital of 20,000 roubles, which had been given by the Russo-American Company in 1823 to help the Yakuts, on account of the great loss of horses they had incurred during the great epidemic then existing, and that this money up to the present time had not been touched, and could be easily used for the construction of a hospital in Viluisk and another one in Verchoyansk. At the same time the Governor said that the money would be only sufficient for a hospital of thirty beds, whereas two hospitals were needed for sixty patients. In 1855 the ispravnick, by order of the Yakutsk Governor, ascertained whether the Yakuts were willing that the money of the Russo-American Company should be used for the construction of two hospitals instead of their receiving the money for the horses they had lost in 1823. In 1857 the Yakuts of the Viluisk and Verchoyansk circuits decided to assign the said capital for the hospitals, but the Yakuts of the Yakutsk Circuit were unwilling to share the expense. In 1857 the General-Governor begged the Yakutsk Governor to find other means with which to build a hospital in Viluisk. In 1860 the Governor of Yakutsk informed the General-Governor that he cannot find other means for the construction of the said hospitals; but, with the money that he hoped to collect among the Yakuts, a new hospital yourta could be built, with all the necessary comforts, for the treatment of lepers. In 1860 they had at last the possibility of building a small shelter for forty lepers in the Sredni Viluisk oulousse; but, owing to the insufficiency of means, this small hospital was closed three years after—that is, in 1863. In

1860, by order of the General-Governor, the Committee of Hospitals in Siberia received of the Russo-American Company's money the sum due to the said Committee for the treatment of the Yakuts during the space of several years. But, nevertheless, the Committee had not the possibility of assigning the sum for the construction of hospitals in Viluisk, Verchoyansk, and Olekminsk, yet, at the same time, consented, in case of hospitals being built in the said towns, to send every year the necessary doctors to treat the lepers. On the 20th of October, 1863, the Cabinet of His Imperial Majesty the Emperor assigned the yearly sum of 3000 roubles for the sick of the Yakutsk Government. With this capital, and the money gathered from the Yakuts, four hospitals were built, which began to work the 4th of October, 1864, in Olekminsk; in Verchoyansk, the 1st of December, 1864; in Kolimsk, the 1st of January, 1865; and in Viluisk, the 20th of October. At the present time—1891—there is a small hospital in Viluisk, with a doctor for eight patients suffering from syphilis. All other patients have no possibility of treatment, although, besides syphilis, small-pox and leprosy devastate the Viluisk Circuit."

Document 2.

" The present existing hospital is very small and dirty, the air is polluted, the patients have neither

linen, bath, nor kitchen. There are eighty lepers said
to be in the Viluisk Circuit; but it is supposed that
there are far more, as the Yakuts try in every way to
hide the disease, being afraid of expulsion from the
community, which always happens as soon as they find
a leper amongst them. The doctors assert that leprosy
is an incurable disease, and not understood, and that it
arises from the condition of the life of the Yakuts. The
immense forests, the endless marshes, the dampness of
the air, the unclean habits of the natives, their food of
rotten fish, water taken from marshes and lakes, the
insufficiency of bread, meat, salt, etc., the famine that
often assails the country—these are the causes of this
frightful disease, slowly but surely killing the people
thus afflicted. Add to this, that the patients of the
two sexes are always together, we can then have
a much better idea of the causes of this horrible
malady.

" The administrative Council of Yakutsk, held in Sept.
1890, found it absolutely necessary to help the population with respect to the medical question, and, as far as
possible, to consider how to better the soil by draining
the marshes, which cover the greater part of this
immense country. The General-Governor Goremikin
coincided with the opinion of the Governor respecting
this question, but decided that, before undertaking such
measures, it was indispensable to study the question of
leprosy on the spot by sending a special doctor, who

would be able to inform them how better to alleviate the future condition of the lepers."

It will be seen, from a careful perusal of these official documents, that, although attempts have been made in the course of sixty-four years to provide a permanent shelter for the lepers, yet, in 1891, no hospital existed specially for them. The hospitals mentioned at the close of Document No. 1 were general hospitals, or for particular diseases, other than leprosy.

A critic of these documents, who is inclined to be severe on official red-tapeism and repeated delays, must remember the great distance of Yakutsk from St. Petersburg (about 5000 miles), and that the transmission of a letter between the two places and back takes many months, and particularly a long time during the breaking-up season. But, notwithstanding any extenuating circumstances, the fact remains that for sixty-four years the lepers of Yakutsk pleaded in vain for a permanent place of shelter. It is enough to make one's heart bleed to read that the hospital opened in 1860 for forty lepers had to be closed three years later, " owing to insufficiency of means." Better had it been for their hopes not to be realised at all, than for the boon granted to be snatched away after three short years.

So, after their brief respite from awful loneliness and misery, these poor creatures were turned adrift to seek again, in the untrodden depths of the forest, the only home which their fellow-creatures would allot them.

Think for a moment what these forsaken ones have to endure in their exposure to extreme cold and intense heat. " Yakutsk is the coldest place in the world. For about eight months in the year the mean temperature is 45° of frost (92° Fahr. below freezing-point). The ground is frozen for thirty feet, and the immense forests are scenes of utter desolation." * The heat in summer is so great that myriads of mosquitoes and flies infest the air, torturing both man and beast, and attacking especially the sores of the lepers, who sometimes are too weak to keep them off. When once a man is known to be tainted with leprosy he is thrust out from his people, and driven away, as if he were some noxious animal, into a lonely spot in the forest, or on the marshes, where he is doomed to a living death. He knows that his disease is incurable, and that return to his friends is impossible. A father, or a mother, a son, or a daughter, full of life and energy, whoever the victim may be, expulsion follows immediately on the discovery of the fatal signs. " No hope! no hope! " is the dread sentence ringing in the victim's ears; and as he leaves his native haunts he knows that never more, perhaps, will a loving face greet him, or kind hands minister to his needs, or the pleasant sound of wife, child, sister, or brother's voice fall upon his ears. He

* Quoted from Dr. Lansdell's Look.

knows he may perhaps have fifteen or twenty years to live—a loathed outcast from mankind. The only shelter he can find is some filthy little *yourta* (hut), which may have been tenanted by another leper, who now, perhaps, is buried near the threshold. His first duty is to make a cross,* which he is bound to place outside, as a warning to any one who may happen to pass to shun him. And so he begins his outcast leper-life—a life so absolutely awful and miserable that none can realise it except a leper outcast like himself.

There are few people, I think, who will hesitate to agree with me that such lepers are the most pitiable and the least cared-for of all God's creatures. Can it be wondered, then, that having, as I humbly believe, a call from God to minister to those whom no one cares for, and having heard of the sufferings of these Yakutsk lepers, I should answer the Divine summons by doing all in my power, in face of every obstacle, to help them?

Having completed my preparations, and being provided with letters of introduction to the Yakutsk Governor, in addition to the letter of Her Imperial Majesty, I set off from Irkutsk. The first and shortest part of the journey we travelled by tarantass. The stage of 235 versts brought us to the River Lena, where we were to resume the journey by water up to Yakutsk. The barge (*pauzock*), which carried us, was little

* See *Irkutsk Eastern Review*, March 10th, 1891, No. 11.

better than a raft, covered over, intended only for transporting goods between Irkutsk and Yakutsk. I had to sleep amongst the cargo, and for the three weeks, which the journey occupied, we had to rough it in every way. I forbear from enumerating the many inconveniences and troubles which had to be borne, and which alone might fill a little volume. How my heart rose in thankfulness to God, on coming near Yakutsk, that I had been spared, after going through so many dangers since leaving England, to see the country in which I intended to work! It was June now. How much had happened in that twelve months of my experience!

On approaching the mainland of Yakutsk, we heard from a native that the Governor had left the town, and that there were no lepers at all in the Viluisk Circuit! The latter part of the statement I knew to be untrue; but the former part quite upset me. It was most important that I should see the Governor; but how was this to be done? The only way out of the difficulty was to go ashore, and, by a short cut through the forest, reach another point of the river, where I might hear tidings of the Governor, or perhaps meet with the boat that was taking him away. The master of the barge very promptly offered to escort me. We travelled through miles and miles of dense forest, with only one narrow road cut through, meeting many of the Yakuts in their strange dress, with high sleeves, just like ladies' sleeves at home. We also met strings of carts, drawn by bullocks, with rings through their noses, and only a collar of wood, and two wooden poles to keep them in their places. As we approached the river again, I saw an ominous appearance of smoke, as if a steamer were starting. We made our little horses tear away, and, on reaching the shore, got into the first empty boat we saw. The steamer was now going at full speed, but our man pushed on with all his might. Then, to my intense satisfaction, I saw the paddle reversed, and knew the steamer would stop in answer to our signals. On rowing alongside, the steps were lowered; I got on board, and saw the Governor, who gave me one of the warmest welcomes it has ever been my good fortune to receive. His account of the lepers was fearful. He begged me to go to them, and said he had made all necessary arrangements for me before his departure. So, after an hour's chat, the steamer speeding on all the time, I scrambled down the side and re-entered that little leaky boat. For two hours we baled and baled, and really that rapid, dangerous Lena seemed eager to draw us into her embrace. It was one o'clock at night, or A.M., according to our ways of reckoning; but it was quite light, and the northern lights, though trying, were beautiful. We landed safely, and, after another little journey, I arrived at last in the town of Yakutsk.

CHAPTER VII.

YAKUTSK—THE PROVINCE—AND THE PEOPLE.

Area and population of Yakutsk—Native traits and habits—
Poverty of the people partly caused by leprosy—Rules of
etiquette—Laying up stores for twelve months—Visit to the
Bishop—Kindness of the Bishop—Formation of a committee for the lepers—"A chiel amang us takin' notes"—
Arrangements for forming the cavalcade to the lepers—My
outfit—The start for the 2000 miles' ride on horseback.

THE Yakutsk province, situated in the far north-east of
Siberia, extends over three and a half million square
versts (nearly two and a half million miles), and contains only 250,000 inhabitants. The population is
made up of different tribes, the Yakuts, a people of
Mongolian origin, forming more than three-quarters of
the entire number. There are about 16,000 Russians,
and the rest of the population consists of several small
nomad tribes, such as the Toungus, the Tchuktes, the
Lamouts, the Youkagirs, and the Tchuvantses.

For administrative purposes the province is divided
into circuits, *oulousses* (a district including several
villages), and *nasslegs* (village communities). There are
five circuits in this province, namely, the Yakutsk, the

Viluisk, the Olekminsk, the Verchoyansk, and the Kolimsk. The town of Yakutsk, with a population of about 7000, is the chief administrative centre of the province, and stands on the River Lena.

The Viluisk Circuit, which interests us the most under the present conditions, extends over 883,000 square versts (about 559,000 miles), and comprises four oulousses: the Viluisk, the Sredni Viluisk, the Marinsk, and the Suntarsky. Forests, marshes, and lakes abound; and along the shores of lakes and rivers there are patches of pasture land which the inhabitants utilise on a small scale for rearing cattle. As no arable land exists, the natives are not agriculturists, whilst fur trading, which is comparatively flourishing in other parts of the province, is here very fluctuating and small.

The natives, even now, are only in a semi-barbarous state, having but recently been brought under the influence of civilisation. In their original state they were idolaters, and at the present time, although considered Christians, they are addicted to many heathen practices. Their abodes are found on the margins of lakes and rivers, where small communities are formed at long distances from each other. This comparative isolation of the communities seems to be a desirable arrangement, owing to the quarrelling propensities of the people. They are also very distrustful, and, therefore, secretive and taciturn; but, nevertheless, they are always ready to give a hearty welcome to a stranger, who may, if he likes, help himself to the contents of the humble larder. Most of the inhabitants of the Viluisk Circuit are very poor, and how some of them continue to exist is little short of a mystery. The fur trade offers a fluctuating source of livelihood ; and many of the people make odds and ends, such as baskets, vessels for food, drinking vessels, ornaments, and cradles out of the bark of trees. Some of these baskets are very pretty, being interlaced with fish scales, which radiate with all kinds of colours. The people live in *yourtas* (huts), of simple construction, for the most part extremely dirty, and devoid of the ordinary comforts of home life. The *yourta* for winter habitation is usually made of light beams, well plastered externally with thick layers of clay and cow-dung.

The poverty of the people, in a measure, arises from the ravages of leprosy amongst the able-bodied. The Sredni Viluisk oulousse is the greatest sufferer in this respect ; and thus the accumulation of arrears of taxes is constantly on the increase. Suntarsky, when compared with the other oulousses, is said to be wealthy, the people being able to build *yourtas* similar to the Russian peasants' *izbas*, and to provide themselves with at least one great domestic comfort—a good Russian stove.

The town of Yakutsk is not a pretty place, and has a dreary, dead appearance. At eight o'clock the houses are shut up, and there are no amusements or recreations. The winter temperature is about 45° of cold, and the air is then filled with mist or fog. The shawl which screens the face is soon covered with a sheet of ice, on account of respiration; the frost also covers the eyelashes, so that it is almost impossible to see at all. Sometimes the cold is so frightful that strong people cannot go out of their houses for days together. It is not light till ten or half-past, and is dark about two; and this state of things continues for nearly eight months out of the year.

The people play cards and smoke, sometimes six hours out of twelve. All the ladies smoke; and the first thing offered to a guest on his or her arrival is a cigarette. The samovar and tea follow, and, whilst smoking, tea-drinking, and talking are going on, the men walk up and down the room the whole time. Never mind how small the room, this constant walking, talking, and smoking all at once is an inveterate habit. The stranger, of necessity, gets somewhat bewildered, until he makes up his mind to feel at home. According to the rules of etiquette, the gentleman must be the first to give his hand to the visitor, who must take off in the hall his cloak, or *shouba*, and fur boots. On no account must the visitor enter the room in his outdoor costume; and if he declines the proffered tea he is guilty almost of a crime. The poorer people use sheets of ice three or four inches thick instead of glass windows, and how they keep themselves warm is almost incomprehensible. Stores come in once a year, and the people must buy for twelve months. There are doctors, but no chemists, and the doctors only buy drugs from Irkutsk once a year.

Soon after my arrival in the town of Yakutsk I went to see the Bishop. We drove in a vehicle called a *dolgushka*, which consists of a few boards, painted a dark colour, placed on wheels, forming a long centre back, the people sit sideways and back to back; it can hold six or eight people, and is considered a superior kind of vehicle. In passing through the broad streets, lined with dilapidated houses, we met a few Yakuts driving carts drawn by bullocks, and sitting on the animals' backs. Their tall hats, long, high-shouldered cloaks, high top-boots, and singularly plain faces looked altogether comical.

In the garden of the Bishop were three churches; and as I mounted the wooden stairs of his house, and entered the small plain hall, the unpretentious look of the place struck me. When His Grace came in, it was impossible not to be attracted by his noble, peaceful face. Devout, unruffled restfulness seemed to be imprinted there; and, as he welcomed me, that peacefulness seemed somehow to influence me. His blue robes, the blue furniture, and the blue paper on the walls, seemed to give him almost an ethereal look; but of course this was only a woman's fancy. He greeted me most kindly. He is very earnest in his work, and does not limit it to Yakutsk only, but sends missionaries thousands of versts up to the north, among the different tribes, to proclaim the glad tidings of Christ's love. His Christianity is practised in all his daily works.

I spoke about forming a committee in Yakutsk; and he at once promised to use every exertion to bring the leading people together, and to help the lepers, not only by relieving their material wants, but also by giving them an opportunity of receiving the consolations of religion. He gave me one of the rare copies of the complete New Testament in the Yakutsk tongue.

On my referring to the herb he said, much to my surprise and delight, that he had a few specimens, and before I left he placed some in my hands. He could give no definite information as to its curative or alleviating properties. It was, however, a source of some satisfaction that the reports I had heard were not altogether groundless. As I was leaving, he came forward and blessed me. Perhaps some friends may think it wrong of me (a Protestant) to receive the blessing of a dignitary of the Greek Church. I took it as a sign of oneness in Christ, notwithstanding wide divergences in creed, and as a mark of brotherhood amongst those working for Christ and in His name. I rejoice to believe that, with our Lord, there is no distinction of church or creed ; we are all one in Him, and He in us. I must add that, during the time I spent in Yakutsk, the Bishop looked after me lovingly and tenderly, as if I had been his own daughter.

Not only from the Bishop, but also from a doctor

in the town, I heard fearful accounts of the lepers in the forests and on the marshes, which were almost inaccessible. The doctor begged me to take tea and tobacco, luxuries unknown to them. I longed to get off, but had to wait for the committee to meet, whilst the preparations for so long and difficult a journey involved a great deal of thought. At last the committee met, consisting of the following members: His Eminence the Bishop of Yakutsk, Meletie; His Excellency the Vice-Governor, Mr. Ostashkin; the Medical Inspector, Smirnoff; the doctor of the district, Mons. Tschevinsky; the doctor of the Yakutsk Hospital, Mons. Nesmeloff; the assistant of the Viluisk police; the tchinovnick of the Governor; the Cossack, Jean Procopieff; and myself.

We discussed the state of the lepers, who had been visited by the Medical Inspector, whose report,* whilst corroborating what I had already heard, supplied additional details of terrible sufferings. Then the question of getting to the lepers came up; and various suggestions were made for my guidance. A plan was prepared of the route I ought to take. But I must refer, in passing, to some difficulties, which I thought were particularly serious for a woman to suffer. Notwithstanding my credentials, a suspicion existed that I was nothing better than a political spy; and it is not always pleasant to find that there is "a chiel amang us takin' notes," which "notes" may be used against one at some

* See Appendix.

future time. It seems to be one of the primary duties of some of the officials in Yakutsk to look out for suspects, and carry a note-book and pencil in their pockets for jotting down any matters which may appear to them of a compromising nature. After some delay, I began buying stores for the journey. I cannot enumerate everything, but only just a few to give an idea of what we thought it necessary to take. Dried bread (almost as hard as a stone, and which had to be soaked in tea before being eaten) packed in fish skins and boxes, covered with fish skin, and, for this reason, smelling and tasting for ever after of bad fish; tea, sugar, tobacco, tinned meats and fruits, biscuits, and an assortment of drugs and an *en-route* basket from Drew & Sons, Piccadilly. What became of most of these things the reader can easily imagine as we continue this narrative.

The Cossack, Jean Procopieff, knowing of my small pecuniary means, and being touched deeply by the sufferings of the lepers, offered, with expressions of sympathy, to lend me all the horses required for the journey as far as Viluisk. He further offered his services as leader of the cavalcade. It was useless to think of travelling by tarantass; such a conveyance would have got wedged fatally in the forest, or would have sunk in some treacherous morass before a single mile had been covered. It was therefore absolutely necessary to make the journey on horseback, and also necessary to employ a number of men not only for

carrying stores, but also as a means of protection against
the dangers to be encountered, not the least amongst
them being the bears, with which the woods are infested.
Our cavalcade was a curious one. It consisted of fifteen
men and thirty horses. The photographer in the town
tried to take our photographs, but the attempt was a
failure, for some one moved during the operation. I
rather shrink from giving a description of my costume,
because it was so inelegant. I wore a jacket, with very
long sleeves, and had the badge of the red cross on my
left arm. Then I had to wear full trousers to the knees.

The hat was an ordinary deer-stalker, which I had
bought in London. I carried a revolver, a whip, and a
little travelling bag, slung over the shoulder. I was
obliged to ride as a man for several reasons—first,
because the Yakutsk horses were so wild that it was
impossible to ride safely sideways; second, because no
woman could ride on a lady's saddle for three thousand
versts; third, because, in the absence of roads, the horse
has a nasty propensity of stumbling on the stones and
amongst the roots of trees, which in these virgin forests
make a perfect network, thus precipitating the unfortunate rider on to the ground; and, fourth, because
the horse frequently sinks into the mud up to the
rider's feet, and then, recovering its footing, rushes
madly along amongst the shrubs and the branches
of trees, utterly regardless of the fact that the lady-
rider's dress (if she wore one) was being torn into

fragments.   For these reasons I think no one will blame me for adopting man's mode of riding, and for making adequate provisions by means of the thick leather boots against the probability of bruises, contusions, etc.

Before starting, the Bishop invited us all to his house for prayer.   He held a special service, praying for God's blessing and protection on our work.   It was a touching sight—this motley assemblage of men, and I the only woman amongst them, receiving the benediction of this servant of Christ on the eve of our perilous journey.

Our object being a very serious one, I took care that as little attention as possible should be attracted by our departure.   All being ready, we set out on the journey of 2000 miles on June 22nd, 1891.

CHAPTER VIII.

FIRST EXPERIENCES OF THE TWO THOUSAND MILES ON HORSEBACK.

What the map says—Sinking into bogs—Camping out—Precautions—Mosquito torments begin—Sleeping in a graveyard—A singular chorus—Visions of home and of the lepers—A very simple breakfast—Siberian thunderstorm—A dead horse and an eagle—Filthy yourtas—Ravages of mosquitoes—A witch-fable—Earth-combustion—Fallen trees—Another thunderstorm—Some results of our shaking—Bear alarms and scaring methods—Food of natives—Frozen corpses—A *yourta menu*—Graves with a tragic history—Keeping my journal—Depression—Arrival at Viluisk.

LET me say to the reader, who at this moment may consult a map of Asia in order to test the accuracy of the statement respecting the number of miles traversed on this eventful journey, that, during the whole of the journey to the extreme points north, east, and west, we were perpetually travelling zigzag fashion, or " tacking-about." This tedious aspect of the journey was rendered necessary partly by the rough and pathless nature of the country through which we had to ride, and partly from the lepers being scattered about, remotely from each other, and quite away from any direct or straightforward course that we have preferred taking. It is true, a post-road from Yakutsk is marked on the map, but only exists in the imagination of the map engraver. The post service, which is not a daily, but only a monthly affair in these regions, is carried on under much the same difficulties which we encountered —along a half-obliterated track—usually; or through forests and over marshes, with no sign of a path, in the best way suggesting itself at the moment.

The Yakut Cossack, already mentioned, led the way: and we had sent on ahead a detachment of the men with the tents, an arrangement which rather made me quake, in case we should lose the men, and have no shelter at night.

At the outset of the journey my " experience " began. We had not gone far when the horses sank up to their haunches in a bog and began to plunge desperately. I had to hold on with all my might, whilst the men yelled at the animals to exert themselves. We rode in single file, and when the Yakut's horse in front partly disappeared we knew there were bogs ahead, and must therefore pick another way. As a rule it was quite impossible to know where one was going. On the borders of the forest we camped for the night. Fires were lighted, tents pitched, tea handed round, horses unloaded and tethered, and then we retired. At the side of each member of the cavalcade lucky enough to possess a revolver or gun, the weapon lay ready, in case of emergencies, the said emergencies referring chiefly to bears. Some men were placed as sentries, and also to keep up the fires.

The next day we started early, and our torments from mosquitoes began. They literally swarmed around us, and, in spite of gloves and a special arrangement for the head and shoulders, my hands, wrists and face became swollen to alarming dimensions. These pests seemed to besiege every crevice where they could contrive to squeeze their bodies in. It was impossible to do much in trying to drive them off, for I dared not let go the reins, which, by the way, were very primitive of their kind and very hard—made of horses' tails—and, before long, wore out my gloves and blistered my hands. All my riding gear, including the quaint Yakut saddle, made of wood—most inconveniently wide—with a cushion fastened on to the top of it, the bridle and reins, and all my own attire I have brought home with me as a curiosity, and also many other things used both in my sledge-riding and horseback-riding, which all speak plainly of the difficulties under which our journey was accomplished.

After a day of seventeen miles, the horses and riders being thoroughly done up, from struggling in bogs and marshes and scrambling through forests, we halted. Much laborious hunting then took place to choose our camping-ground. The men selected a deserted grave-yard, and wishing, I suppose, to find a specially cosy spot for me, they pitched my tent at the foot of an old grave; but I did not remonstrate, although I feared there was little chance of peaceful sleep. The cuckoo gave us a welcome, and the Siberian nightingale —very unlike the English—entertained us for hours; but the neighing of the horses, as they were bitten by the mosquitoes and large horse-flies, sadly interfered with the musical greeting. All around dense clouds of damp were rising from the sodden soil; and, when I closed my eyes, visions of home, with its clean soft beds and snug rooms, sprang up, quickly replaced by the dreadful vision of the outcast lepers, starving, and dying in misery. Of course, I had to sleep in my travelling clothes, not even taking off the heavy boots. Having been stifled by heat, tormented by insects, almost saturated by the moisture of the air, and plagued with nightmare, I awoke and had breakfast, which consisted of tea and hard bread soaked in it.

At an early stage of the journey I experienced my first forest thunderstorm; and the lightning in Siberia, by its great volume of fire, seems as if bent on making a rough-and-ready compensation for the brevity of the Siberian summer. The flashes were awful, the rain came down in a deluge, and we took refuge (very foolishly, I suppose) under some trees. But we soon got soaked, for our waterproofs were on ahead, and there was no time to get them. The hot sun began to shine, and quickly dried us; and, to my astonishment, no one took cold.

Before long we had another diversion. We came upon a large number of birds of many kinds, flying about in all directions, and uttering shrill cries and plaintive wails. The Cossack raised his hand to attract our attention; and then we saw a dead horse; the tchinovnick whispered, as he came up, " Eagles ! " The Yakuts stealthily got off their horses and crept into the forest; but the eagle was too sharp for them. After proudly surveying us as if we were inferior mortals, and making a few graceful movements, he flew away, conveying in his claws a pigeon, and dropping, what a Yakut found to be, a leg of a large rabbit. The man secured the leg as if it had been a great prize, saying, " I can't refuse such a luxury, hunted and caught for me by the king of birds."

We arrived at one of the few post-houses in the full blaze of a tropical midday sun, intending to rest for a few hours. Oh, that station house, how it seemed to reek with filth ! A man and a woman kept it; and their garments were so dirty that they could never have come into contact with soap and water throughout their long existence ! Two calves occupied one end of the room, and the primitive fireplace poured out clouds of smoke. We had tea, dried bread, and a piece of tongue; and then, in spite of all drawbacks, went fast asleep on one of the wooden benches in the hut.

More bogs and marshes for several miles; and then I grew so sleepy and sick that I begged for rest, notwithstanding our position on semi-marshy ground, which had not as yet dried from the heat of the summer sun. I was asleep in five minutes, lying on the damp ground with only a fan to shelter me from the sun.

On again for a few more miles ; but I began to feel the effects of this sort of travelling—in a word, I felt utterly worn out. It was as much as I could do to hold on to the horse, and I nearly tumbled off several times in the effort. The cramp in my body and lower limbs was indescribable, and I had to discard the cushion under me, because it became soaked through and through with the rain, and rode on the broad, bare, wooden saddle. What feelings of relief arose when the time of rest came, and the pitching of tents, and the brewing of tea ! Often I slept quite soundly till morning, awaking to find that the mosquitoes had been hard at work in my slumbers, in spite of veil and gloves, leaving great itching lumps, that turned me sick. Once we saw two calves that had died from exhaustion from the bites of these pests, and the white hair of our poor horses was generally covered with clots of blood, due partly to mosquitoes and partly to prodigious horse-flies. But those lepers—they suffered far more than I suffered, and that was the one thought, added to the strength which God supplied, that kept me from collapsing entirely.

Sometimes we rested all day, and travelled at night to avoid the intense heat. We passed forests, where hundreds of trees had fallen. According to popular superstition, the Yakut witches quarrelled, and met in the forest to fight out the dispute. But the spirit of the forest became so angry at this conduct that he let loose a band of inferior spirits; and then, in a moment, a tempest began and rushed through the forest, tearing up the trees and causing them to fall in the direction of those disputants who were in the right. But the true meaning of those fallen trees is yet more interesting and singular than the superstitious one. Underneath the upper soil of these forests combustion goes on, beginning in the winter. The thaw of summer and the deluge of rain seem to have little effect upon the fire, for it still works its way unsubdued. When the tempest comes the trees drop by hundreds, having but slight power of resistance. I brought home with me some of this burnt earth, intending to send it to the British Museum, should no specimen be already there.

My second thunderstorm was far worse than the first. The forest seemed on fire, and the rain dashed in our faces with almost blinding force. My horse plunged and reared, flew first to one side, and then to the other, dragging me amongst bushes and trees, so that I was in danger of being caught by the branches and hurled to the ground. After this storm one of the horses, carrying stores and other things, sank into a bog nearly to its neck; and the help of all the men was required to get it out. Those stores! I may say now, that long before the journey was accomplished they were nearly all spoilt or gone, thus adding to our already accumulating difficulties too numerous to particularise. Hard bread became flour, and we had to make a kind of cold pudding with it.

Soon after the storm we were camping and drinking tea, when I noticed that all the men were eagerly talking together and gesticulating. I asked the tchinovnick what it all meant, and was told that a large bear was supposed to be in the neighbourhood, according to a report from a post-station close at hand. There was a general priming of fire-arms, except in my case, for I did not know how to use my revolver, so thought I had better pass it on to some one else, lest I might shoot a man in mistake for a bear. We mounted again and went on. The usual chattering this time was exchanged for a dead silence, this being our first bear experience; but we grew wiser as we proceeded, and substituted noise for silence. We hurried on, as fast as possible, to get through the miles of forests and bogs. I found it best not to look about me, because, when I did so, every large stump of a fallen tree took the shape of a bear. When my horse stumbled over the roots of a tree, or shied at some object unseen by me, my heart began to gallop. However, all our preparations were wasted, for the bear remained conspicuous by his absence; and, when the danger was passed, we all became very brave and talkative. We had a few simple devices for scaring away bears as we rode through the forest later on. The men used to sing and shout their hardest; bells were placed on some of the horses, and we had tin boxes half filled with stones in one hand, which we continually shook, thus making a great clattering noise.

I can just imagine how some brave bear-hunter will laugh in his sleeve, as he reads this simple mode of keeping off the ferocious creatures, which had just woke up ravenous from their winter's sleep. But, you see, we were not hunting for bears, but searching for lepers, which makes all the difference in the world. At one point some natives told us they had just seen eleven bears; but happily, although we noticed significant foot-marks, we saw none of the fraternity. Sometimes I almost felt I would rather be eaten by bears than endure the terrific clatter and noise made by the cavalcade.

Some of the natives in these wild parts eat the bark of trees mixed with milk, and now and then fish or birds. Bread, even black bread, to many is an unknown luxury. Milk is often sold in blocks; fish, meat—in fact everything—is frozen.

The burial of a native in winter is a long process. The ground has first to be thawed by placing fires upon it for three days and nights. Those who are buried at this season remain frozen always, and their bodies continue in good preservation for hundreds of years.

At a yourta, where we stopped, quite a grand dinner was provided for us—some black meal, fried like pancakes, sour cream, tea and milk, and a dish of fish caught in the summer and kept frozen ever since. I was thankful for a rest in that yourta, notwithstanding the suffocating smoke arising from a burning heap of cow-dung in the middle of it. The aperture at the top for letting out the smoke had been covered, this plan being the only means of protection from the incessant assaults of the mosquitoes and flies; but I leave you to imagine the effect of this rough remedy on one's eyes, head, and throat. I ached in every bone, and trembled all over, and was too tired to pay any attention to mosquitoes, fleas, bugs, &c.

We passed several graves on our way, some of them containing, so I was told, the bodies of murdered people. When I looked upon those little mounds, I half wished that I, too, was at rest. There is a point of exhaustion reached at times when one wishes for nothing else than complete unconsciousness.

Whenever I was not too tired, I made rough entries in my journal before going to sleep, and sometimes suggestions, as they occurred to me, for the leper hospital or colony that I had in my heart. But when constant pain brought on fits of depression, I felt that I should never live to carry out any of my cherished plans. But these were only momentary weaknesses, for the very dangers and difficulties I was going through without serious accident proved so clearly that God's loving arm was around me, shielding and protecting me, and would surely lead me in safety to the end of my work.

I have not sufficient space to enumerate all the difficulties and troubles of this first part of the journey as far as Viluisk, but have said enough to give an idea of our experience. Pushing through forests, plunging into bogs, camping at night, plagued with mosquitoes, sleeping at times in disgustingly filthy yourtas, which swarmed with vermin of many kinds, myself more than once so wearied and aching that I could not dismount, having to be dragged off the horse, my clothes sometimes wet through with rain, with no possibility of taking them off to be dried; after such experiences, I at last arrived at Viluisk.

Here the kind Cossack, John Procopieff, who had been our guide, bade us good-bye. Before leaving, he presented me with an address of farewell and good wishes. Feeling sure that this quaint, kind-hearted letter will interest my readers, I will here insert a literal translation. At the end of it the writer gives his testimony to the hardships of the road, which are dreaded even by the natives, born and reared in the country, and consequently accustomed to them from their childhood. Also, at the end of this book, will be found a literal translation of an account I wrote in French about the journey, and which the interpreter read and signed as an eye-witness of it all. I thought that, as

Yakutsk and Viluisk were so many thousands of miles away from all civilisation, and so inaccessible, any one might easily think my account was perhaps only a traveller's tale, and somewhat exaggerated; and this was my reason for having Russian official documents for every statement made.

A MEMENTO TO MISS KATE MARSDEN, FROM THE COSSACK, JOHN PROKOPIEFF, WHO ESCORTED HER FROM YAKUTSK TO VILUISK.

"Viluisk, July 3rd, 1891.

"You, the much honoured friend of the suffering poor, in visiting this distant land so far away from the civilised world, with the only aim of helping the unfortunate lepers, convince the population that our Mother of all Russians, our Most Gracious Empress, has approved you for so great a work, as the best example of self-denial on behalf of others. These are more in need of help than any other subjects of her Imperial Majesty. There can be no doubt about your purposes being noble and holy, when you are protected in your work by our most Gracious Sovereign, Mother of the poor, needy, and suffering. My prayer to the Almighty Creator is that He may grant you the possibility of carrying out your good intentions to the end, and thus better the methods of alleviating the disease of the lepers.

"Love to one's neighbour is the Creator's holy will;

and, therefore, your work, which is founded on this commandment, is sure to gain its own good end. May I ask you to accept my greeting, Sister of Mercy, and Mother of the needy.

" With the earnest wish that you may obtain those better remedies, which would give you the possibility of signalising your coming here, by a glorious attaining of your good purposes, and thus show the population and the world that your self-sacrifice is an example to do good to mankind, even outside your own country, and your enduring such privations as would even frighten a native, accustomed and hardened in childhood to the difficulties encountered in the ways of communication.

" Retired Cossack of the Yakutsk—Cossack—Town Regiment,
" JOHN STEPANOFF PROCOPIEFF."

CHAPTER IX.

MISERIES OF THE LEPERS.

General appearance of Viluisk—One doctor to 70,000 population—
Father John Vinokouroff—Committee, and consultation—
Looking for a site for a hospital—A midnight repast—Site of
former hospital—Story of a supposed child-leper—Demoralisa-
tion of lepers in filthy *yourtas*—Leper's garments—Setting off
to a leper settlement—The mother and her leper-boy in the
forest—Marking tracks for the journey—A motley group.

VILUISK is one of the quietest places I ever visited.
It is provided with what are called "roads," which are
quite overgrown with grass which seems never to have
been cut since the town was first made. The cows and
horses turn the roads into their pasture ground. No
one is ever in a hurry, and all the people take life
easily, just as it comes to them. There are two
churches, or rather, one in course of erection, and
another which is much in need of repair. The prison
is small and contains twenty-five inmates. It was feared
that a visit from me might rouse a suspicion that I
was connected in some way with the political prisoners
there, and, if such a suspicion arose, my work for the
lepers would at once have come to an end. So I

thought it wiser not to visit it. There is only one *droshky* in the place, and that belongs to the town priest. The Ispravnick, who is the leading man of the place, has no less than 70,000 people in his circuit, under his control, scattered over a district larger than the whole of France; his salary, however, is only £100 a year. There is only one doctor, with two assistants, to these 70,000 people, even though, according to Medical Inspector Smirnoff's report, epidemics and famine frequently break out, with scarcely the possibility of alleviation.

We were met at Viluisk by Father John Vinokouroff, who is an earnest Christian man, and devoted to the lepers. He frequently goes amongst them, fearless of contagion, simply to minister to them, and to speak of the Saviour's love. From him and from other persons I learned additional details—worse than those contained in the Medical Inspector's report—of the frightful condition of the lepers in the province. I was assured that they were thrust by the community into immense forests, with barely anything to cover them, and that, in many cases, they were closely packed in dirty *yourtas*.

After meeting several of the leading Yakut people of the town, and consulting about plans and prospects, we visited the site which had been proposed for the much-needed and longed-for hospital. On account of the intense heat, we deferred starting until evening. Father

John, the *feldsher* (doctor's assistant), a merchant, and two Cossacks went with me. We had about twenty miles to ride, chiefly through forests, and found on arriving that the place proposed would not do at all for the hospital. I think the meeting we held that night, to discuss the *pros* and *cons*, was about the most singular one I ever attended. It was midnight, but not dark; and we were all seated on the ground in the tent, partaking of refreshment as we talked. The refreshment consisted of a goose, cut up into small pieces, which were put into a large plate. We helped ourselves to the tasty morsels with our fingers, for knives and forks had been forgotten, and only one or two plates had been brought. Much amusement was created, and on the whole the meeting, or midnight picnic, as, I dare say, some people would call it, proved a light and innocent little diversion from the serious business that weighed upon our minds.

The poor lepers are so looked down upon as the very dregs of the community, that, even those wishing to befriend them, have fallen into the way of thinking that the worst is good enough for them. Thus, when the question rose about materials and workmen, it was very hard for me to impress upon the people the necessity of having the very best in both cases, not only on account of it paying in the end, but because I so wanted to make these poor sufferers realise that it was our Lord who was sending help

to them, and, therefore, He could only send them
the best.

The next day I visited a spot where a hospital was
built some years ago, but which had to be closed for
want of funds. There was nothing left except a few
stumps in the sand to mark where it stood. The
Yakuts who went with us would not even stand upon
the ground, so great is their terror of the awful disease.
This site was also unsuitable for the new hospital, the
forest having been cut away, and there being no shelter
or pasture ground for the cattle.

Whilst gathering all the information obtainable about
the lepers, I learned from an official Russian document that some people suffering from other diseases
were often exiled with the lepers, and compelled to
remain with them as such, owing to the mistakes made
by the natives when defining leprosy. I was also told of
instances of inhuman brutality being practised in the
name of leprosy, in order to obtain some small fortune
from a relative. When once any one becomes a leper
all right to property passes away from him. I soon
heard a heart-rending illustration of this feature of leper
life. Information was received at Viluisk, two years
before my visit, that a supposed child-leper had been
starved to death. After an investigation, the true facts
of the case became known. This child's father and
mother died and left him a few cows. His uncle took
charge of him and his sister, and at once began to

practise upon him unheard-of cruelties. After murder-
ing the sister, he conceived the inhuman plan of getting
the community to believe that the boy was a leper, in
order to secure the cows. His plot succeeded, and he
at once drove off the lad into the depths of one of the
densest forests in the district, where, in truth, the only
inhabitants were bears. This occurred in the midst of a
Siberian winter.

The uncle had formed a kind of kennel in which
the child was to pass the rest of his days. It was
made simply of a few sticks thrust into the ground,
lightly covered with cow-dung and snow; and there
the child was left to starve, or to be frozen to death.
What his sufferings were can scarcely be conceived. It
would be impossible for him to find his way back,
through this trackless forest, to his uncle's place.
Without food, without warmth, with only five hours'
daylight out of twenty-four, frightened by the sounds
of wild creatures, shaking with cold, and startled by the
fierce winds howling in the forest, driven to the verge
of madness, this poor child passed at last into God's
keeping.

The rest of the story I quote from the official police
report. " I found," says the *feldsher*, "a place not
large enough for a dog. On the floor there was a little
straw, the outside was covered with cow-dung, snow,
and earth. Just a few yards in front I noticed a place
in the ground freshly moved, and, on scraping away

some snow, I found the dead body of the child, not placed in a coffin, but just covered over with earth. It was the body of a skeleton; I opened his stomach and found only a little clay which he had eaten ; the body was perfectly healthy otherwise; there was no disease and no sign of leprosy."

Such a story needs no comment from me. It must surely appeal to the heart of every reader, especially to mothers. To whatever nationality you belong, let me remind you, oh! gentle mothers (who would rather die a thousand painful deaths than a little one of yours should be subject to such cruelty), that it is for you to prevent, by your unflagging interest, sympathy, help, and prayers, the occurrence of a similar instance of wrong-doing anywhere in the world.

I must add, in justice to the Russian authorities, that the miscreant—the author of all this suffering—was arrested, after considerable difficulty, and condemned to several years' imprisonment.

I also learned how the lepers become utterly de-moralised, by the men, women, and children herding together in the same filthy yourta. They live like animals, and with animals, for even the cows dwell in the same hovel. The consequence of this de-moralisation found vent not long since by a jealous woman-leper killing a man-leper in a most horrible manner.

The Yakuts send their cast-off clothing to the lepers ;

but these garments, generally fur skins, are not given away until they can be worn no longer by the owners. They are filled with vermin, filthy beyond description, and often nothing but a mass of rags.

Where the lepers herd together, they themselves bury their dead, and the priest goes once a year to read the prayers over those who have died during the year.

One of my journeys from Viluisk was to Mastach, where I was to have the first sight of a real leper settlement. The first ten miles had to be done in a boat, and the rest of the distance on horseback. In one part of the forest, where every sign of life seemed to have departed, we suddenly came upon a yourta, and near it a fire made up of branches of trees. Being tired we stopped and sat down near the fire to keep off the flies and mosquitoes. In a few minutes we saw something moving amongst the low shrubs of the forest. Gradually the figure of a woman appeared, who was only half-covered with filthy rags, and who, having heard of our coming, had lain in the shrubs watching for us. Near her was her son, a lad of fourteen. Her tale of woe was soon told. Her son was supposed to be a leper. The head of a neighbouring tribe, having decided that he was infected, condemned him to be separated from his mother, and to live alone in the depths of the forest, ten miles away from any other hut or human being. After being in the forest some time, he became so maddened by the torture and misery of his solitary life, that he begged his mother to allow him to come at night and sleep near her. She consented, and made a small room at the back of her hut, into which he crept every night. But the fear that his shelter would be discovered and the indulgence stopped kept him in a constant state of alarm. I arranged with the chief that the child and his mother should be protected, and the boy permitted to remain with her. I can never forget the terrified appearance of that boy as I went near to touch him; he at first flinched, expecting that I meant to hurt him. Even after being at the place for some time, he still shrank when I went up to him. He was made to think himself shunned and dreaded by every one, and was bound to retire and keep as far away as possible at any one's approach. The shrinking of that child would have touched the most callous heart; it spoke such volumes.

To give a further idea of the difficulties of travelling in these parts, the natives had to cut a path for me, and mark it, through swamps, by sticking long poles in the ground, and putting a large piece of earth on the top of each. This had been done for 1500 versts.* Where they made a way through the forests, they chipped a large piece off the trees at a distance of about twenty yards.

* See Viluisk Ispravnick Antonovitch's letter to me (Appendix).

We were quite a motley group. There were the ispravnick, four starostas, and about twenty Yakuts, all mounted on horseback, wearing their strange native costume—high shoulder pieces, handkerchiefs of all colours covering their heads and hanging down their backs. The wild, ungroomed, unkempt horses added to the singularity of the scene.

CHAPTER X.

AMONGST THE LEPERS.

A treacherous forest path—Amongst the lepers at last—The lame,
the halt, and the blind—Distribution of stores—Indescribable
filthy condition of the lepers' yourtas—Living with the
dead—A healthy girl for eighteen years with the lepers—A
Russian's noble offer—Lepers to have new yourtas—Perils of
the return journey—Alarms from bears and wild horses—A
leap from the river—An unpleasant walk through the forest—
A good sleep for a weary one.

WE wended our way through the forest along the 1500
verst-track that the Yakuts had so readily and lovingly
marked for us; for they did this work of their own will
and without remuneration, though to accomplish it they
had to lay aside their summer work in the fields. They
knew whither we were bound, and this was the proof of
their sympathy for the mission and their pity for the
lepers.

Although a path had been marked out for us, the
stumps and roots of trees had been left. We rode over
a carpet of half-decayed roots, all interlaced with one
another. Now and then my horse sank, not this time
in mud, but into holes, well hidden amongst the roots,
getting his feet entangled in such a way that only a
Siberian horse could extricate himself. I had to hang

on to the saddle, my body ready for every lurch the horse might give in freeing himself, and prepared to help him at the right moment. We went through miles and miles of forest like this.

At last I thought I could discern ahead a large lake, and beyond that two yourtas. My instinct was true to me; and the peculiar thrill which passed through my whole frame meant that, at last, after all those months of travelling, I had found, thank God! the poor creatures whom I had come to help. A little more zigzag riding along the tedious path, and then I suddenly looked up and saw before me the two yourtas and a little crowd of people. Some of the people came limping, and some leaning on sticks, to catch the first glimpse of us, their faces and limbs distorted by the dreadful ravages of the disease. One poor creature could only crawl by the help of a stool, and all had the same indescribably hopeless expression of the eyes which indicates the disease. I scrambled off the horse, and went quickly amongst the little crowd of the lame, the halt, and the blind. Some were standing, some were kneeling, and some crouching on the ground, and all with eager faces turned towards me. They told me afterwards that they believed God had sent me; and, my friends, if you could all have been there, you would no longer wonder at my having devoted body and soul to this work.

I at once ordered the things to be unpacked, and had them collected on the grass. A prayer of thanksgiving

was then offered by the priest, and, next, a prayer for
her Imperial Majesty the Empress, in which the poor
people heartily joined.   As we distributed the gifts,
some of the distorted faces half beamed with delight ;
whilst others changed from a look of fear to one of
confidence and rest.   Surely such a scene was worth a
long journey, and many hardships and perils.

They seemed to know that help was coming, and that
although they might not live to enjoy it, other afflicted
ones would.   The poor fingerless hands, and all the sad
contortions with the stamp of hopeless misery on every
face—even where a flickering smile had appeared—
made me shudder.

The condition of the yourtas is best described by my
quoting the documents of two officials, who were sent
there by the Government.

The medical inspector, Mr. Smirnoff, says, in his
report * to the Governor: " One is struck at the sight
of the smallness of these nomad huts, in which they
dwell.   Light hardly penetrates, and the atmosphere is
so infected by the conglomeration of the lepers, and
the exhalations of rotten fish, that one is quite suffocated
on entering them.   These unfortunates have neither
beds nor linen ; their clothing consists only of sheep
and cow skins, all in rags, and it is under these conditions, without any change, that they are obliged to live
tens of years, till at last death releases them from their

* See Appendix.

sufferings. Not far from these huts one perceives graves with crosses on them, indicating the places where the lepers bury each other. The door is so small that one is obliged to bend to be able to enter. The hut is very low, and hardly any light enters, and the atmosphere is so foul that even the fire which is continually burning in the fireplace cannot purify it. The filth of this hovel is disgusting; the dirty table and the few benches covered with filthy skins, in lieu of beds, comprise everything in the place. I found six men and three women huddled together in this infected hovel. It is inexplicable how so many people get to be lodged in so small and low a hut. The clothes of these lepers consisted of skins (of cows) all in rags and holes."

The tchinovnick for special services, Mr. Shachourdine, in his report, contained in Protocol No. 3, states:— "The interior of these yourtas is not known to me, as, however much I wanted to get acquainted with the interior of the said huts, I could not get into them, on account of the fearful stench, similar to that coming from a dead body; which was due not only to the lepers themselves, but also to the food that they ate, consisting chiefly of rotten fish."

The yourtas, swarming with vermin of many kinds, were made out of the trunks of trees, fastened with wooden nails, and covered with cow-dung, of which the floor also consisted, mixed with earth. The windows were only one foot square, and were covered with calico.

The lepers have no beds. Round the inside of the yourtas were placed trunks of trees, upon which were fixed pieces or planks of wood. On these the lepers slept, closely packed as near to each other as possible, the feet of one to the head of the next. Men, women, and children were all mixed together; calves were also kept there in the summer, and cows during the winter. There was no kind of sanitary arrangements; and, sometimes, in the depth of the winter, none of the inmates venture outside for days together.

In this place the lepers eat, cook, sleep, live, and die. If one of them dies, the body is kept in the hovel for three days. The smoke fills the place—stifling both the lepers and the cattle. Not long ago they had small-pox amongst them, and four of their number died, and the dead bodies were kept in the same yourta for three days. The dead are buried only a few yards from the dreadful abode, so that the lepers cannot pass their threshold without being reminded of the end daily drawing nearer.

This is but a faint description of what I saw; I have exaggerated nothing, and all I have said can be confirmed by the ispravnick or the priest, who live in Viluisk.

Amongst the lepers was a girl of eighteen, who was perfectly free from the disease. Her mother, being infected, was sent off to the yourta, and, before long, gave birth to this girl, who thus had been here all her life—for the Yakuts would never allow her to go amongst them. She pitifully implored us to take compassion on her, and remove her from this horrible place. We held a consultation, and the ispravnick said he was resolved to break the spell of terror that ruled amongst the Yakuts, and then nobly promised to take the girl into his own house as servant. I scarcely knew how to express my admiration of this splendid conduct. All who try to appreciate the full significance and after-effects of the brave chief's decision will not hesitate to class him amongst those whose hearts have the true ring of heroism, and of that charity which is the essence of the Christian religion.

Our return journey was a rather eventful one. My horse became restive, pricked up his ears, shivered and stood still. It was not without much coaxing that I could get him to move. Then other horses became restive, but we managed to go on through the silent forest. The tchinovnick rode forward and reported that he saw a bear crouching in an ominous manner. We were badly armed, there being only two guns and one revolver amongst all the thirty of us. We went on quickly for some distance and then encamped. I was lying down in my tent trying to sleep, but, in reality, wide awake planning the hospital, when suddenly I heard a tremendous stampede—a crashing of branches, horses neighing, and, altogether, a great clamour. I fully expected to see that bear march boldly into my tent; but he had been content, it seemed, with frightening the horses. We started again, and every one was on the alert, feeling sure that the bear would follow us; the cunning fellow might spring from behind a tree at any moment, and the stories I had heard of the doings of these creatures in the woods were not calculated at that moment to fortify one's nerves.

Crash, crash, crash! The horses reared—I got off mine, preferring to meet the bear to being dragged through the forest on a mad horse and dashed against the trees. Evidently the bear was somewhere at hand, for one of the baggage horses had flown into the thick of the forest, and was jammed between two trees, causing all this commotion. A little later, whilst we were resting, another of these baggage horses took fright. Its tail was tied to the bridle of another horse, and it dragged its neighbour round and round an open space, the baggage bumping against its hind legs. Then all the other horses got restive, and in another moment would have torn away into the forest had we not quickly quieted them. These untamed Siberian steeds often proved a source of danger to our limbs and lives.

Other alarming incidents occurred, but I will only mention one more. We had to row about twenty versts up the stream, but were unable to make headway against the rapid current. A terrific storm began, and, as the violent gusts tore across the water, they forced the boat against over-hanging trees, and sometimes against the high bank. And whilst we were in this predicament the men shouted, yelled, and screamed as if they were a lot of madmen. The ispravnick managed to get on shore; and I began to think it was high time I did something for self-preservation, for a tumble into that river would have been the end of me. So I quietly watched for an opportunity, and then jumped ashore. The tchinovnick followed, and then we set off to walk ten miles through the forest, one, it was said, in which no human foot had ever been before. Having been without sleep for twenty-four hours, and not having broken my fast for twelve, I was not in exactly good training for that pedestrian feat. I got on tolerably well for about three miles, and then simply dropped. Again I struggled on and again dropped. My very indulgent and patient escort were getting a little tired of this sort of thing, so some of them went forward and sent back two or three soldiers to help me. These sturdy fellows had to drag me into Viluisk, whilst pain seemed to rack every atom of my body. Then I went to bed and slept for twenty-four hours. That rest was, indeed, a godsend, for we had to start in two days on a journey of a thousand versts.

CHAPTER XI.

THROUGH FIRE.

A girl's gratitude—A leper's woeful story—A weird scene—
Choosing the site for a hospital—Pathetic appeal of the
priest—Pushing through the forest—Another leper settlement,
and its dreadful condition—Sending off lepers into the forest
on bullocks—A midnight march—Naked lepers—Stumbling
onwards—Forest solitude and the screech of owls—A devoted
husband—Child-lepers—A startling spectacle—The earth in
flames—Picking our way through fire—-A mad horse and a
narrow escape—In God's hands—My little collie guides me—
Exhausted.

WE left Viluisk on the evening of July 27th (August 8th)
for our next journey of about 1000 versts.   Among the
crowd who came to see us off was the girl from the leper
settlement whom the ispravnick had taken into his house,
and who, with her new clothes and beaming face, looked
a different creature altogether.   In spite of my attempts
to stop her she would insist on prostrating herself in
her native fashion, so unbounded was her gratitude.

We had to travel by boat for the first few miles of
the journey ; and at midnight we landed for a rest in a
kind of wild arbour, where a number of men were
waiting for us round a log fire ; behind us was the

dense impenetrable forest, silent as death. At some distance was another fire ; and, on my asking presently why there were two fires, the men told me in an awe-struck whisper that a solitary leper, having heard that I was passing, had come to beg for help, and had waited patiently. This second fire was kindled for him, as the men were too frightened to allow him to share theirs, and had not ventured to go near him.

I got up and hurried to the poor fellow, who actually cried when he saw I was not afraid of him ; and, kneel-ing, touched the ground with his forehead to express his gratitude. These prostrations, expressing their gra-titude, were a sore trial to me ; but, do what I would, I could not prevent them, being unable to speak to the people in their own language ; and at last I was obliged to submit, as I was told it was a native custom, and by objecting to it I would wound the feelings of the people. Then he told his sad story, the priest acting as inter-preter. He was dressed in filthy rags, and had lived for years, alone and despised, in a dense forest. It was indeed a touching scene ; there he stood, half frightened, despair depicted on his face, his rags scarcely holding together, the flickering fire giving him a weird appear-ance, and the branches of the trees in the background forming a slight shelter. We gave him what help we had brought, and comforted him by the prospect of a colony, where proper care would be taken of him, and where he would be fed, clothed, and kept warm ; and we asked him to pray that the Lord would soon grant us the means to erect it. On returning to the men they shrank away from me as if I, too, were contaminated.

We rowed thirty miles farther down the river, and then stopped to choose the site for the future leper colony. It is away from the villages, but within easy reach of Viluisk, so that the authorities will have immediate supervision of the hospital.

Another row brought us to the place where we were to mount our horses to reach Sredni Viluisk, a distance of about fifty miles, and where all the heads of the district were drawn up ready to receive us. The priest got on shore first, and in a few minutes I followed. These few minutes were rather lengthy, I am afraid, for the bank was steep and high, and climb up it alone I could not; so the Cossack at the top had to get hold of my hands and pull, whilst the one in the boat helped up my feet, and thus, with their united help and my own exertions, I was landed.

Here occurred a little scene for which I was quite unprepared. The good priest was so overcome with gratitude at the efforts being made to relieve the lepers that he fell on his knees before me, tears running down his face, saying that it was God who had sent me to help these poor sufferers, who had been burdening his loving heart for so many years. He implored me to use every effort so as to bring my plans to a speedy result, promising to pray for blessing for each step of my way, for, truly, I had come to help the most miserable of human beings. Before this I had heard of his devotion to the lepers, but now I fully realised what a deep God-given love he had for them. My prayer went up to the Healer and Comforter of all afflicted, to strengthen and protect this earnest and simple servant of His in his devoted ministrations, begun and continued to His glory, and His only.

Whilst resting under a very picturesque shelter, made of branches of trees stuck into the ground, and which had been prepared for us by the Yakuts, we discussed the plans for the hospital and the needs of the lepers. Then we mounted and rode off, twenty-five men and myself, with thirty horses, some of them carrying baggage.

We pushed our way through the usual dense forest, along the track which had been cleared for me by the kind natives, as I have already mentioned, and which otherwise would have been impassable. Halting at the leper settlement of Hatignach, a scene met my eyes too horrible to describe fully. Twelve men, women, and children, scantily and filthily clothed, were huddled together in two small yourtas, covered with vermin. The stench was dreadful; one man was dying, two men had lost their toes and half of their feet; they had tied boards from their knees to the ground, so that by this help they could contrive to drag themselves along. One man had no fingers; and the poor stumps, raised to make the sign of the cross, were enough to bring tears to the eyes of the most callous. On my approaching them they all crouched on the ground, as if almost terror-struck at the very idea of any one coming near to help them. I gave them all the help possible, and then, with a smile on their faces, they looked and pointed heavenwards, trying to make me understand that they were praying for blessings on those who had considered their wants. In some cases the fur of the tattered clothes had stuck to the sores, thus causing intense irritation.

During the eight or nine months of winter, these people huddle together with the cattle as closely as possible in their dreadful hovels, in order to keep warm. They, too, had been attacked by typhus fever and smallpox. I said farewell, and, mounting my horse, heard angry words behind me. Turning round I found that some of the lepers wanted to come near to speak to me, and the Yakuts were driving them away in horror, fearful lest they might catch the disease. Of course, I quickly went to them. They pleaded hard that the hospitals might be built speedily, and that they might be supplied with bread, because the food brought to them was generally putrid.

Then we set off for the next settlement, which was a hundred and fifty miles farther on. We travelled all night—in fact, the greater part of this journey had to be done by night on account of the intense heat during the

day, and the incessant attacks of large horse-flies, as well
as the myriads of other insects.   We halted at Sredni
Viluisk, which, although marked as a town on the map,
is only a collection of a few dirty yourtas and one
Government office.   A man suspected of being a leper
was brought to me, and, after examination by the doctor,
the suspicion was soon confirmed.   It was arranged that
he should have a new yourta, and live at a leper settlement about fifty miles away.

"How is he to get there ? " I asked ; for I saw how
deformed he was, and that parts of his feet and hands
were gone.

"He is to walk," was the reply.

This walking meant that the poor fellow would have
to crawl or drag himself along fifty miles of forest.   At
last, it was suggested that he should be tied to the back
of a bull, and the bull to be led by a boy (the man's
brother) with a long cord.   After a deal of persuasion
I got the people to provide a sledge, with plenty of
straw, and a bull to draw it, as there were no horses to
spare.   This is only a typical example of how some of
the lepers, almost unable to walk at all, are left to get
as best they can into the far-off forest.   If a woman
becomes a leper, she, too, is sometimes placed or tied on
a bare-backed bull, which is led by a man with along
rope.   If the animal sinks into the marshes or bogs, it
must struggle out without help, and if the woman falls
off, the man would rather die than go and touch her in

giving assistance. Such sufferings as these, I try to refer to calmly; but it is hard to do so. The reader can imagine, without my help, all that such outcasts are compelled to endure. What a difference the bare-backed bullock presents to the merciful contrivances for removing the wounded from the battle-field and the victims of accidents in our streets!

Another dreadful instance of what they had to endure was related to me. A leper woman was placed in a yourta with another leper, a man, who, soon after her arrival, became insane. For four years this poor woman had to live with a madman in the depth of the forest, away from every human being, never sure from one hour to another of her life. Just picture the constant dread she must have lived in—at night, hardly daring to close her eyes to sleep; during the day, ever on the watch for each movement the man made, knowing well that, should he attack her, there was no hand to protect her, no ear to attend to her cries for help—for miles and miles around nothing but the dense forest to echo back her voice. As, bit by bit, this information was translated to me, a tremor went through my whole being; whilst, deep in my heart, I thanked God for sending me here to these helpless, forsaken ones.

Our midnight march from Sredni Viluisk was beset with dangers. We heard that bears were in the neigh-bourhood, and the horses kept on starting, and then darting to one side and the other. The trees loomed above us against the sky, the rotten roots and holes were under our feet, and on every hand was a dead silence.

After a long ride we came to nine more lepers, whose condition was worse than any I had seen. Two women, one man of about forty, and two children were naked, having no clothes whatever; and, with the exception of a few rags, they are in the same state in the winter. During the months of biting frost, all the covering they had was hay and rags. As I sat there amongst them, the flies were tormenting their festering wounds, and some of the outcasts writhed in agony. I do not wonder at being told that it was impossible to reach the lepers, for this was another settlement hidden away in the forest, with no path or communication of any kind to other places. There were traces of a bear here, and I began to wonder why some of these lepers did not, in their desperation, throw themselves in the way of the bears, and so end their miseries.

As we again mounted our horses, the Yakuts, who had kept far off from the lepers for fear of contagion, hurried on the animals in order to get away from the place as quickly as possible. As we rode forward in the darkness, the faces of those poor creatures haunted me ; whilst now and then an owl hooted, or a savage rat darted at my horse, making him plunge and struggle. We kept stumbling into holes and over roots of trees, and it was as much as a tired, aching woman

could do to keep her seat.   Then two of the horses took
fright; and, all the horses being tied in single file by
tail and bridle, the whole cavalcade rushed along full
tilt into the darkness, and we were simply at God's
mercy.   When we went steadily again, and silence
reigned around, how my full heart was lifted up to
God!   When going at full speed, the horses would
suddenly stop; then a wild goose would screech and
flutter his wings, and on we would tear again.

At another place I found a yourta, too small even for
one man, containing a man, two women, and a child.
One of the women had been afflicted with leprosy in
all its worst aspects for years; she was almost naked,
having only a dirty strip of leather over her.   By her
side was her husband, who, although free from leprosy,
nobly determined to share his wife's exile.   Her child,
too, preferred to accompany her mother rather than
remain with the tribe.   Neither husband nor child will
ever be allowed to enter the community again.   Close
by was a woman who had just been confined.   And
there were also two children here, born of lepers, born
to live amongst lepers, and doomed most likely to
become lepers, either from contagion or hereditary taint.
Surely some definite steps ought to be taken to alter
this state of things.   According to Medical Inspector
Smirnoff's report,* who had visited the lepers three
months before me, he had ordered the separation of the

* See Appendix.

men and women to be carried out. But, however, when I was there, I found them all together again.

The next night, as we proceeded on our journey, a scene occurred which will never be effaced from my memory. A more graphic pen than mine is required to paint it in all its weird and alarming details. We had been travelling for about twenty miles since leaving the last place, when I noticed how strangely the horses' tread sounded—just as if they were walking over a tunnel, with only a shallow roof to it. The tchinovnick explained that this was one of the places where the earth was in a state of combustion. The fire begins a long way below the surface, and burns slowly, still more slowly when there is no vent for the smoke. The burnt earth creates great hollows, and there is always danger of a horse breaking the crust and sinking into the fire. I thought little more about the matter except speculating on the causes of this alarming phenomenon in the bosom of Mother Earth.

Night came on, and all was gloom around us. By and by I thought I saw in the distance several lights; going on a little farther the lights became a glare, and then my horse grew restive and almost unmanageable. We emerged from the forest and stood in an open space. What an unearthly scene met my eyes! The whole earth, not the forest, for miles around seemed full of little flickers of fire; flames of many colours—red, gold, blue, and purple—darted up on every hand, some forked and jagged, some straight as a javelin, rising here and there above the earth, and, in places, seeming to lick the dust, and then, having gained fresh energy, springing as high as the others. A full description, signed by the tchinovnick, who acted as interpreter during the journey, of this phenomenon is given at the end of the book. Coming, full of nervous apprehension, out of the dark forest on to such a scene, I half fancied that those flames were endowed with life. The lurid spectacle looked like a high carnival of curious creatures, let loose for a time from their prison-house, careering about in fantastic shapes. Blinding clouds of smoke every now and then swept into our eyes, and the hot stifling air almost choked us.

We had to go through the fire; there was no escaping it, unless we chose to turn back. After looking on, aghast, for some time, and trying to prevent our terrified horses from bolting, we moved slowly forward, picking our way as best we could in and out of the flames. I prepared, as well as I was able, for any emergency, slipping my feet to the edge of the stirrups in order to release myself in case of an accident, then tightened the reins, and followed my guide. I never expected to get through that fire alive; but death was better than turning back. Slowly and cautiously we picked our way, whilst the horses snorted, hesitated, and trembled.

All went well for about three miles. Suddenly we heard an ominous, crashing noise behind, and then a loud cry, which was instantly taken up by the whole cavalcade. We stopped our horses and waited for the worst to happen. In a few minutes there came, dashing at full speed into the midst of us, a poor frightened baggage horse, which, stepping into a hole, had taken fright and darted away, the baggage boxes getting loose and thumping against its hind legs as it tore along. It made straight for us, and, in another moment, would have thrown me and my horse to the ground, had not the tchinovnick deftly turned the mad creature aside. Then the poor thing bounded on and went far ahead, and we heard the boxes crashing against half-burnt trunks of trees. All our horses were straining at the rein, and seemed bent on starting off wildly after the one that had disappeared; but we gradually soothed them, and then pushed on. The smoke was still blinding us; and, not being able to see in the least where I was going, I loosened the reins and just let the horse go where he liked.

Soon we entered a splendid forest; and, coming from vivid light into darkness, the darkness to me was blackness indeed. My horse kept stumbling, and first one branch and then another hit me in the face. I again dropped the reins on to the horse's neck, put up my arms to shield my face, and left all in God's hands. As my eyes grew accustomed to the pitchy gloom I could see the white tip of my dog's tail. I quite forgot to mention this faithful friend before. He was an ordinary sized black collie, with a white tail. I knew that he always followed the Yakut guide, who rode in front of me; so I kept my eyes fixed on that little bit of white, and felt that, as long as I could see it, I was tolerably safe; if the white spot disappeared I knew we were near a hole, and so must be prepared for an accident.

Complete physical exhaustion came at last. I had never been on a horse before, except once, for a short time, several years ago; and after all these weeks of riding on a hard saddle, with little sleep and food, and all the perils and alarms of the journey—well, it was time, perhaps the reader may think, that I did get exhausted. So I had to rest, and I began to feel symptoms of an internal malady, which at first alarmed me; and I thought I might have to die there in my little tent, and leave, only just commenced, all the work I wanted to do. But the Master's presence cheered me and banished all depression. A day's rest, and then I started again, although in great pain, which, unfortunately, lasted till the end of the journey.

CHAPTER XII.

FINISH OF THE TWO THOUSAND MILES' RIDE.

A sagacious dog—A leper for twenty years!—Burial of lepers—
Father John on the condition of the lepers—The doctor thinks
I need attention—Another faithful dog—A leper's appeal—A
night of horrors—Baptism of a leper's child—The Medical
Inspector's Report—The Holy Communion—My last "spin,"
and how I re-entered Yakutsk—Farewell to my escort—
Letter of the ispravnick—The Bishop's kindness again—A
valuable letter—Journey up the Lena—Arrival at Irkutsk.

IN one place, where there were several lepers, I
found that, when starving and pushed by hunger, they
would leave their yourtas, the weather permitting,
and drag themselves to the nearest village, and there
stand crying out until the people brought them food.
An instance was related to me of a leper woman
who repeatedly made her way, as well as she could,
to the village to steal food. The starosta heard of
the matter, and, wishing to put an end to the visits,
ordered all her clothes to be taken from her, so as to
prevent her leaving the yourta. But the pangs of
hunger were too strong; and one day the unfortunate
woman ventured out clothesless, despite the winter

and was found, some days after, lying frozen under a tree.

Here, too, small-pox had been making ravages; and another trouble of these outcasts arose from bear-alarms. The crashing of these creatures through the forest made the lepers shudder, dreading an attack and swift destruction. They had an intelligent dog, however, who seemed to know how to manage the bears. On their approach to the yourta, he used to dance and bark, and, backing into the forest all the time, gradually lured the beasts on and on for miles, and then, suddenly leaving them, would return home by another route. This story of the dog's instinct and fidelity was told me by the lepers themselves, and I have no reason to doubt its truth. I was struck by the patient endurance of these lepers. They had no word of complaint to make against any one, but simply prayed that help might be sent quickly.

At another place I came to a small yourta, in which were two women lepers, one child, with the cattle in the yourta. As I stepped into the darkness, the stench took away my breath, although I was now so accustomed to the horrible condition of yourtas, and I had to move back into the fresh air.* One of the women had lived here for twenty years! Her feet had rotted up to the ankles, and all she wore was a filthy fur jacket. She told me a fearful story of what happened in cases of

* See Appendix (Protocol No. 3), p. 208.

death. I shrink from repeating it; but my account would be far from complete and accurate if I omitted some of the most harrowing features in my experience amongst the lepers. At the same time, I beg the reader to understand that some of the worst details are too repulsive to write about, even for the sake of increasing sympathy on behalf of the lepers. Let it also be understood that all I have said has been verified by others; and, whenever space will permit, I intend quoting from signed documents.

This woman said that, when one of her miserable companions died, the Yakuts sent a coffin in a sledge, and left it at some distance from the yourta. In her diseased and mutilated state she had to drag it into the yourta and prepare it for the reception of her companion, whose corpse remained in the yourta for three days. Then she had to get the body into the coffin without any assistance, drag the load across the floor, lift it over the threshold, and push or drag it away, getting it somehow into the sledge; and there she left it for the Yakuts to bury.

Dr. Smirnoff, in his official report to the Governor of Yakutsk (the greater part of which is given in the Appendix) of his visit to the lepers in the beginning of 1891, states that, in some settlements, the lepers have to bury each other, the graves being marked with crosses.

Here I may quote from the paper signed and pre-

pared by Father John, of Viluisk, on the condition of
the lepers: "On the whole of the earth you will not
find men in so miserable a condition as the Sredni
Viluisk lepers. The name 'leper' is used by the
Russian tchinovnicks who are sent for service into the
Viluisk circuit as a 'swear' word. An illustration of
the intense dread the natives have of leprosy is their
conviction that it originates from the devil. 'Small-
pox, measles, scarlet fever,' they say, 'were appointed
by God; but leprosy was sent by the devil.'" Hence
their belief that all lepers are possessed. Father John
also makes a number of other statements; but as they
would be simply a repetition of what I have already
written, I abstain from quoting further. Extracts from
his statement will be found in the Appendix, and they
corroborate many of the details which I have given
in this book.

Having resumed our journey through the forest, I
became so ill after a few miles that we had to halt. I
doubt if any of my readers have ever experienced such
utter exhaustion of both mind and body; my hands
literally refused to hold the reins. There lay the reins;
I knew they had to be held, but I was totally incapable
of communicating any power to my hands. Added to
this, I was suffering acute pain from an interior abscess,
which the constant riding had formed. Seeing me
sway from side to side on the saddle, the tchinovnick
came up and stopped the cavalcade. The men lifted

me off the horse, laid me on a rug on the ground, and in a moment I fell into a dead sleep. I awoke in a half-dazed condition, found all the horses tied to the trees, the tchinovnick driving off the mosquitoes from me with a horse-hair whisk, and the ispravnick and the feldsher looking at me anxiously. They began to think that something ought to be done for me, that, in fact, I was too ill to go any farther. But I told them that they were giving way to unnecessary alarm, for I had asked the Lord to let me finish this work, and was trusting Him to strengthen me step by step; so I persuaded them to lift me on to my horse, and was soon on the move again.

After a ride of some twenty miles, we came across a lonely leper, who had lived in the forest for six years, with no companion but his faithful dog. This dog, like the other I mentioned, was his master's guardian against the bears. He seemed to smell the bears in the distance, and then dashed off to tease and tantalise them, leading them away and away, and then returning to his master voiceless and half dead. No word of murmur came from this man's lips; he only appealed that the hospital might be quickly built; and we left him with his eyes lifted up to Heaven in prayer.

A few miles farther we came to a forest which had been recently burnt. Its blackness stood out in sharp contrast to an adjacent vast desert of sand. We stayed for the night close to the forest; and I think, as the

tchinovnick also thought, that, in its horror, that night
came next to the night of burning earth. Screeching
owls and wild ducks, eagles keeping the small birds in
a state of terror, the wind whistling through the trees,
and the branches cracking and crashing as they fell—
all this clamour drove sleep from our weary eyes.

Again we started and had to endure forest troubles
and swamp troubles similar to those already narrated.
At the next leper settlement the soldier had considerable difficulty in getting me off my horse. I was
suffering from cramp, and therefore almost powerless.
A little rest brought me round again partly, and then I
went forward to see the lepers. A man and a woman
here could only crawl on their knees, and they had
but a little girl of six to help them. They were not
married, and the child was not baptized. After a deal
of persuasion we got the priest (not Father John) to
baptize the girl, and she was afterwards removed to a
distant place in order to be out of the reach of contagion.

Farther on there was a woman-leper who had lived
quite alone for six years, dying by inches, never hearing
a human voice except when the man who brought food
shouted to her a hundred yards from the yourta. She
had to crawl through the deep snow to fetch the food,
obliged to make several journeys, being able to carry
only one thing at a time.

The medical inspector states in his report, already
referred to, that the authorities, and the inhabitants

in general, endeavour to settle the lepers in so-called "dead" places, "unfit for the use of the healthy, and at the same time as far away as possible from all other habitations, roads, tracts and footpaths." He further says that "food is provided for these unfortunate people by the community once or twice a week, and consists of meat, fish (in various forms), often sour and rotten, tea and milk. It sometimes happens that the food is not brought to them at the appointed time, and the patients have to suffer from hunger for two or three days; but these cases are rare.

My catalogue of leper miseries, as seen with my own eyes, must now come to an end, lest I weary the reader with scenes which, in most of their dreadful aspects, greatly resemble each other. This round of visits ended appropriately, as I thought, by the priest administering the Holy Communion to three or four lepers at one of the yourtas. Being a Protestant I could take no active part in the service, and yet I felt that the living presence of our Lord was amongst us, for we were gathered together in His name, and He seemed to say, as the poor, weary, dim eyes of the lepers brightened for a moment, "Inasmuch as ye did it unto the least of these, ye did it unto Me."

During the rest of the return journey to Yakutsk, we rode about seventy miles a day, with little food and sleep; at times we were in a dense forest, and seemed to lose our bearings. The feldsher proved a friend in need; he provided us with fresh food by shooting the wild ducks we came across, which were very acceptable, for we often had only dried, black bread left, two months old. As to water, small stagnant lakes were our only resource. The colour was dark brown, and the odour abominable; and yet we hailed it as a friend, and drank it as only thirsty people can drink. How it was we were not all killed by imbibing such liquid is a marvel to me to this day.

More struggling and floundering through marshes and bogs, more pitch-dark forests, bear-alarms, and frightened horses, and then a terrific thunderstorm. Frightened horses again; swimming head and exhaustion; my poor tired little steed sinking into mud and water, and stumbling into holes as awkwardly as ever. I cling to his flanks for dear life; a plunge into that morass would be the end of me. Wet to the skin, I am dragged from the horse and made to stand by a fire to get dry; but I drop on the ground and go to sleep in spite of screeching owls and ducks and everything. On again: and I sway from side to side, backwards and forwards, my cramped knees refusing to do as I wished, whilst the tchinovnick calmly begs me to hold on and keep steady. With my head as dull as a lump of lead, and my hands nearly powerless, I tie the reins round my wrists and let the horse do just as he likes. This sort of equestrianship fails to please my escort; so a cart is hired, a layer of hay placed at the bottom, and I am placed above it; and thus, after a twenty miles' jolting, I re-enter Yakutsk, like a wounded soldier after battle.

And now, with many regrets, I had to part with my escort. I need scarcely speak of my great indebtedness to all the worthy men, from the tchinovnick down to the Yakut guide, who went with me on that long journey. Their steadfastness and readiness to do all that I required are sufficiently obvious throughout my account of the 2000 miles' ride, and need little praise from me now. They were chivalrous and devoted, without exception. I was always at their mercy; but never for one instant did they betray the confidence reposed in them. Two things kept them staunch and true—that a woman was entrusted to their care, and that they were bound on a mission of mercy to their outcast brethren. May God ever bless them for all the help they gave me!

The noble-minded ispravnick handed me, on parting, a farewell letter, which I cannot forbear from printing:

Letter of the Viluisk ispravnick Antonovitch. His farewell address to Miss Marsden, 31st July, 1891.

"Miss Marsden,

"Having come to the limit of the circuit in my government, and having thus finished the special and extraordinary commission of my chief to accompany you and protect you through your journey to the different places where the leper dwellings are to be found, I deeply regret to be obliged, by the duties of my service, to bid you farewell and to return to Viluisk. But, before expressing to you, Miss Marsden, my sincere and quite special respect and heart-felt esteem, I beg of you to allow me to say a few words about the importance of your visit to the Viluisk Circuit, but especially to the Sredni Viluisk oulousse. Her Imperial Majesty the Empress, who is always thinking about the good of her people, having informed you about the intimations that had reached Her Imperial Majesty concerning the sad condition of the unfortunate lepers of the Viluisk Circuit, and getting to know your desire to inspect them, has graciously deigned to allow you to personally witness their sad condition and truly unbearable and deplorable position, and to get acquainted with the local means of treatment of leprosy, if such exist, and also to determine the best way in which a hospital could be constructed for them. How far it is necessary to build a hospital you have now been able to judge for yourself. You have yourself seen sixty-six lepers in twelve different places, that is, almost all the lepers officially known as such in the circuit. What can I add to your own personal impression? The purport of these words is only to direct your attention to how terrible a scourge leprosy is for the whole of the population, but especially for the Sredni Viluisk oulousse, where it seems to have its nest.

"Having had the government of this circuit for more

than three years, and, before that period, having served
in different offices in the same circuit, I have constantly
had the question of the deficit of their domestic economy
before me as due to leprosy.   Each new victim to this
disease deprives the community of the Yakut nasslegs
not only of a workman, able to pay his own taxes, but,
besides that, obliges them to maintain him at their own
expense, as well as the whole of his family, who, in him,
lose their only means of support.   The inhabitants of
the local community are obliged by turns to carry the
food to these lepers, who are so scattered and at such
long distances, that, in doing so, they lose a lot of time,
and are put, as well, to a great deal of work.   The
community have such a dread of leprosy, that, when
any one of them falls ill, they are ready at once to sus-
pect the symptoms of this disease; in consequence of
this they are ever on the watch, and have often-repeated
inspections and meetings, with the one purpose of
defining whether one or the other of the community is
a leper.   On receiving the news of your arrival at
Yakutsk, and the directions given by His Excellency
the Yakutsk Governor about taking all possible means
to alleviate the frightful and difficult journey you were
undertaking, I went at once to the Sredni Viluisk
native administration and collected all the chiefs of
the nasslegs and representatives of the population.   I
informed them that the sole purpose of your journey—
almost impossible for a woman, especially for one who,

like yourself, has been accustomed to every comfort—
was to alleviate the position of the suffering lepers, and
to organise a hospital for them. You cannot imagine
with what deep gratitude and inexpressible joy they
received this information. As a vivid testimony of this,
was the way in which they unanimously set to work to
clear a road through the forest for 1500 versts along the
Viluisk Circuit, which I suppose you noticed, and which
would have been impassable during the summer. They
made little bridges across the marshes and the
dangerous parts of the bog, and set about this work
with so much earnestness, that they threw aside their
own summer agricultural work, and, altogether, tried to
make some kind of a road so as to enable you and your
baggage to pass along without being hurt. The expression of their wish to take you through on their own
horses shows how well they understood and realised
the good which you have wished to do them, by coming
to visit the lepers, and the good results that they know
will follow for the whole of the population—thanks to
your self-denial.

"Again, at several of the places where you stopped
for rest, the Yakuts assembled in full body to express
their heart-felt gratitude for the kind and truly Christian
work that you have undertaken for the alleviation of
their unfortunate sufferers, which will also be of such
utmost importance as regards the good of the whole of
the Sredni Viluisk oulousse. At the same time, on

their knees, they asked you to lay at the feet of Her Imperial Majesty the expression of their true and loyal feelings, as well as their tears of gratitude for the solicitude shown by Her Imperial Majesty for her loyal servants the Yakuts.

"Miss Marsden, in bidding you farewell from the depth of my heart, will you allow me to have the honour of kissing your hand, which has done so much good to the population committed to my charge? Wishing you every success, and trusting that you will finish your journey in good health, at the same time allow me to express the hope that God may yet grant me the honour of seeing you again in this life, with deep respect and devotion, I have the honour to remain,

"Your humble servant,

"N. ANTONOVITCH.

"July 31st, 1891.
"Kobaisky Nassleg of the Sredni Viluisk oulousse."

On reaching Yakutsk I went straight to bed and slept for twenty-four hours without waking. It was hard work to get my limbs to move after this little rest, my body was so bruised and sore and aching, whilst from my waist to my feet I was black and blue.

Before leaving for Irkutsk, I had the pleasure of again seeing the kind Bishop of Yakutsk, who gave me a pastoral letter in recognition of my visit to the Yakut lepers. In it he states that I had ridden over

3000 versts in seeking the lepers.   I was glad to know
this from a man of his authority, knowing the country
well, whereas the Yakuts have only a confused notion
of distance, and could never tell me the exact number
of versts.

The translation of this letter is as follows : —

" *To Miss Kate Marsden, Sister of Mercy.*

" DEAR MADAM,

        " Moved by a feeling of sympathy and pity for
the poor lepers of the Yakutsk Government, you have
accomplished an unparalleled deed of charity by coming
to visit them from England and St. Petersburg, so as to
see their sad condition, and at once take measures to
alleviate their fate.   By God's help you have already
accomplished this journey, having visited the Viluisk
district, overcoming unheard-of obstacles along the road.
What with the dangers, the risks to your own health,
the pain and difficulty of riding on horseback for over
3000 versts and the frightful contagiousness of the disease, you came to them with your fellow-travellers like
angels from heaven to comfort them.   By your true
sympathy in their sorrow, your material help in their
need, and by the promise of building them a refuge,
you have raised their fallen spirits with the hope of a
better and brighter future.   I feel bound to send you
this, my pastoral letter, dear Madam, as an expression

of my sincere gratitude for your self-sacrificing work of Christian love, praying for God's blessing to rest on the beginning of this your good work. May He continue to bless it, and thus help you to carry out your good intentions of establishing a refuge for the lepers.

"Humbly yours,

"MELETIE.

"Bishop of Yakutsk and Viluisk.

"Yakutsk, August, 1891."

My journey up the Lena towards Irkutsk was accompanied by just as many inconveniences and difficulties as I experienced on my outward journey. I was exhausted and ill on the voyage, and had to lie in my berth, half dazed, all day long. During the evening I sometimes crawled on deck, looking at passing boats and the scenes on the banks. To add to the discomforts, about 150 men from the gold mines, with wives and children, joined us. Babies crying, and men and women quarrelling, were bad enough; but the fearful smells were worse to endure. When the river became shallow, we had to change into small post-boats, which, though covered at the top, are exposed to rain, wind, and fog at both ends. We were short of provisions, and for five days we lived on eggs, potatoes, and tea. Sometimes we grounded on the mud, or on stones, and then, as the men hauled us off clumsily, and we tumbled about, I began to wonder how long it would be before we were all at the bottom.

On landing, I had to finish the journey by tarantass, so there was more bumping and jolting.

On arriving at Irkutsk, I went to a quiet, clean hotel, which, though an unpretentious little place, was, to me, quite a luxurious palace after all I had gone through.

CHAPTER XIII.

HELP FOR THE LEPERS.

Progress at Irkutsk on behalf of the lepers—Dangers from robbers—A trusty soldier—Contributions for the lepers—Departure from Irkutsk for Tomsk—My tarantass collapses—The riches of Siberia—Preparations for the Grand Duke's journey — Post-station keepers—Swindling drivers — "Once bit, twice shy"—Perils from trains of baggage-carts—My narrowest escape from death—Discomforts of low sledges on muddy roads—Arrival in Tomsk and visit to the convent—Volunteers for the relief of the lepers—Duties of sisters and nuns—A doctor volunteers—The proposed colony for the lepers—Peasants' horses and houses—At Tjumen again—The railway once more—Ufa and Samara—Arrival in Moscow.

On the morning after arriving at Irkutsk, I had to call on the General-Governor, who, at my request, summoned the committee to hear an account of my visits to the lepers. The committee consisted of His Excellency the General-Governor, the two Archbishops, an aged priest, Mr. Sievers, the doctor, the inspector, Captain Lvoff, and myself.

I read a *résumé* of my travels, and begged hard for help for the lepers ; I asked, first, for warm clothing, and, thank God! about £150 were at once contributed for that object.

When the question of building a hospital arose, a great deal of discussion ensued, principally on account of the necessary funds.

However, when I informed them of my intention to plead with all the leading people of Moscow and St. Petersburg on behalf of the lepers, and, if possible, lay the sad state of their existence before Her Imperial Majesty the Empress—but that I hoped the Siberians would come forward and help their own outcast people first—the General-Governor then said that he would do all in his power to get sufficient money to build four large temporary huts, where the lepers could be sheltered, to provide them with cows, and to endeavour to obtain contributions towards the hospital.

Shortly after, a sum of £1000 was contributed, which was left in charge of the governor.

Fully realising that, had I known the Russian language much more could have been collected, nevertheless, I was deeply grateful to our Lord for this good beginning, and rejoiced to think that the poor unhappy people would, at last, have a decent place to live in, proper clothes, and good milk to nourish them.

The General-Governor, who was most kind, gave me an order to visit the vast central penal servitude prison at Alexandrovsky, where there are 3500 prisoners; thus some of my time was again taken up in visiting prisoners, distributing tea and sugar, and giving copies of the Gospels.

I was very thankful to have the protection of a soldier, who always slept at night on a rug outside my door. Notwithstanding his guardianship in the house, a thief entered a bedroom close to mine one night and stole 700 roubles. When I add that my room was on the ground-floor and could easily be entered from the outside, also that during my week in Irkutsk there had been more than one murder committed, it can well be imagined that my trusty sentry contributed considerably to my peace of mind. The kindness and courtesy of both the soldier and the aide-de-camp of the General-Governor, who was also appointed to look after me, were undeviating. I have already expressed my admiration of Russian soldiers; and the high opinion of them was confirmed again and again during my travels.

I left Irkutsk in October for Tomsk, a distance of over a thousand miles.

Looking back upon the results of the few days I had spent in Irkutsk, I praised God for the help He had enabled me to get for His lepers; and prayed for further guidance at each step.

Now that the first contributions had been given, God would send others, and my next special prayer was for earnest Christian women to be found, who would be willing to go and nurse the lepers, as well as others to do the menial work.

We travelled in a tarantass, which, at an early stage
of the journey, broke down, the front wheels giving way.
It was, altogether, a very awkward business; but we
managed to get another vehicle, and off we went
galloping again.

Siberia is doubtless one of the richest countries in
the world; but its untold wealth lies in the earth
almost untouched. If only English or American
enterprise could be imported there, Siberia would be
turned, literally, upside down, and the veins of rich ore
be brought to light. Then would come the flourishing
days of gold and silver, as well as of milk and honey.

A great change had taken place in many respects
since my outward journey towards Yakutsk. The
Grand Duke had been making his tour, and, to prepare
for his coming, old bridges had been repaired, telegraph
poles repainted, and post-stations scraped, scrubbed,
cleaned and white-washed. But all the white-washing
in the world would fail to rid the stations of vermin;
there they were, still crawling placidly over walls and
everything, in spite of Imperial mandates for their
extirpation by lime and water. If these noisome
dwellers in the stations were an everlasting nuisance
to me, provoking repeated complaints in the course of
these pages, some of the poor keepers of the stations,
who would have banished the pests if they could, earned
my gratitude in more ways than one. I knew just
twelve words of Russian, and, with that meagre voca-

bulary, I had to try and make my wishes known at every station. But these keepers, instead of laughing at the stumbling and stuttering of the foreigner, did all they possibly could, by persistent dumb motions and so forth, to get an inkling of my meaning. And sometimes, when I tumbled out of the tarantass, looking like a bundle of dirty rags, and stepping ankle-deep into thick mud in the darkness, these poor fellows would show all sorts of little kindnesses, which I most heartily appreciated.

My diminutive Russian vocabulary was insufficient now and then to save me from extortion at the hands of keen-witted drivers. Once, when the interpreter had left me in order to attend to some work at a distant place, I found I had paid for seven horses instead of four, the number harnessed to the vehicle. I did not wake up to the fact that a swindle had been perpetrated until I had gone through a series of arithmetical calculations between the one station and the next. And when the next station was reached, those Jehu fellows actually tried the same trick! But I was too sharp for them this time. I sat down, wrote " four " on a scrap of paper, then held up four fingers, and shook my head when I saw them exchanging knowing looks, which meant a conspiracy to extort the price of seven steeds. Then they shouted and yelled, but I kept cool and waited; and it is astonishing the effect that English coolness has on the Russian temper.

Hoarse muttering gradually succeeded to the shouting, and at last I got four horses at their proper price. The trick was *not* tried at the next station.

More than once my tarantass became almost hopelessly intermixed with trains of baggage-carts. This kind of predicament used to begin with a sudden outburst of yelling, rather alarming in the pitch darkness; the cart-drivers seemed to try and bring their horses and vehicles right under the noses of our horses; there would be a general scuffle and muddle; then my driver would go off to exchange compliments with the other drivers, leaving me alone, wondering what would happen next.

Before reaching Tomsk, I had one of the narrowest escapes from death that ever fell to my lot. It was a bitterly cold night; now and then from amongst broken, dark clouds the moon shone brightly. After a day's rain the frost had come, making the roads like a sheet of glass, except for the holes which frequently occurred. We had to climb and descend several steep hills, and as we flew down, at a terrific speed, I became a little nervous, particularly as the driver was quite a youth, and therefore apt to be venturesome. But, being exceedingly tired, I fell asleep, notwithstanding bumping and jolting. On awaking I found we were at the top of a mountain, and the driver was in the act of tieing one of the wheels preparatory to descending. All went well for a time; but presently the horses began to go faster and faster, and suddenly, when we came to a hole in the road, the driver was pitched amongst the three horses. I sprang to my feet and tried to get hold of the reins, but found that the driver had twisted them securely round his wrist. And there was the poor fellow being tossed to and fro amongst the legs of the horses, which, now terrified, tore down the hill like mad creatures. I was perfectly helpless either to save the doomed driver or myself. There was nothing to do but to breathe a prayer, and wait for God's will to be done. In a few minutes there was a fearful crash. We had come into collision with another tarantass, and the six horses and the two tarantasses were mixed up in a chaotic mass. The interpreter and I jumped out of the vehicle and searched for the driver. There he was, all but dead, half crushed under a wheel ; his horrible, ghastly condition I dare not describe. As for myself, I felt like one snatched from the jaws of death, whilst I knew it was only by God's mercy that I had been preserved from the fate of the poor young driver.

During a portion of this journey I had to ride in a low sledge, which is pictured in the illustration. I had to partly lie, and partly sit, whilst the driver stood in front of me, in danger of being thrown back upon me, should the sledge happen to bump into a hole. If such an event occurred (and it did occur), the horses, of course, became alarmed, and there was a general scramble amongst driver and horses to set themselves right again. If a thaw began, and the road became muddy, there was no protection for me against the stones and mud thrown up by the horses' hind feet; and sometimes I was literally covered with mud. In going down hills it was useless to tell the driver to be careful: my caution seemed to have an effect just the opposite to the one I desired. I knew that, if over-turned, I should probably be dragged along, face down-wards, over the stones, and, perhaps, kicked to death by the horses. This kind of travelling was bad enough by day, but by night it was considerably worse; fortu-nately, but a little part of the journey had to be accomplished in this primitive fashion, and that only in the breaking-up season, when none but those on urgent business travel.

My return visit to Tomsk was a very memorable one. I arrived in November, 1891, and, after much deliberation and prayer, visited the convent. The Abbess received me very kindly; and when I described the condition and wants of the lepers, both she and all the sisters were deeply affected. Self-sacrificing women were needed to go to the lepers—would some of these sisters volunteer? I asked earnestly for God's guidance, and then felt that it was my duty to appeal to these women to devote their lives to the service of the lepers. So I went again to the convent, and begged the mother in Christ's name, and for Christ's sake, to undertake the mission. When I ceased speaking, she calmly and deliberately said, "Yes, in His name, and for His sake, I will do it."

This promise was made conditionally, on permission being obtained from Mr. Pobedonostzoff, Head Procurator of the Synod.

And here let me explain the difference between trained nursing sisters and nuns in Russia. The sisters are generally drawn from the middle and upper classes. They are specially trained in hospitals in nursing the sick, and form quite a separate institution or community. There are several important communities of this kind, both in St. Petersburg and Moscow. One, in the former city, was started some years ago by an English Quaker lady, and is in every respect a model establishment. It is now under the patronage of the Prince of Olden-bourg, one of Russia's great philanthropists. But the nuns are, for the most part, peasant women, robust, and inured to hardship, and accustomed to all kinds of manual labour. It is their duty to attend to the domestic matters of the convent, cleaning the premises, baking bread, preparing meals, making candles, etc. They are also able to attend to slight repairs and renovations, such as glazing, papering, painting, and are further employed in tilling the ground, and gathering in the crops.

General Tobiesen, the good governor of the town, took me one day to the University of Doctors. I wanted to interest these professional men in the lepers, and took with me a specimen of the skin of a leper—which, at my request, had been taken from the lepers I had visited by the feldsher (assistant surgeon), who accompanied me—for scientific examination. I gave them an account of what I had seen, and a detailed history of some of the leper cases. Then, on asking that one of them would go and study the disease on the spot, once the colony was erected, my request, much to my joy, was granted. I stipulated, as I had also done in making my request to the mother, that he should not have to encounter the dangers that I experienced, and that the lepers should all be collected in the colony, which I hoped to establish.

Before continuing the story of my journey, I must bear grateful testimony to all the kindness, sympathy, and help accorded to me by General Tobiesen and his family. Nothing could exceed the friendliness, and the anxious desire which the General displayed to second all my efforts ; and, indeed, the many proofs of his kindness of heart, and of his wishfulness to overcome difficulties for me, form one of the pleasantest recollections of my Russian travels.

In travelling from Tomsk to Tjumen, I found that Government horses were so few, and the delays, in consequence, so many, that I decided to hire peasants' horses. This alteration necessitated my putting up at peasants' houses instead of at post-stations.

The Siberian peasants' dwellings are, as a rule, beautifully clean; but my favourable opinion was destined to be somewhat qualified during this portion of the journey. On arriving at night at these houses, I would find hay covering the ground, and the head of the household, his wife and children, and two or three men, asleep on this very primitive kind of bed; and I had to join them. The room would be in a state of dirtiness and stuffiness almost enough to stifle and poison one. The same experience occurring night after night, I went back latterly, in sheer desperation, to the post-stations and the Government horses. Let my unpleasant experience be a warning to travellers to avoid patronising peasants' houses.

At last I arrived at Tjumen in a rather lamentable condition. What with exposure to bitter cold and tropical heat, and all the fatigues of the previous months—with the jolting, broken rest and little food—I was now, vulgarly speaking, "done up." I was sore in every joint, frightfully exhausted, and, even with a comfortable bed and surrounded by kind friends, I could get no sleep. Mr. and Mrs. Wardroper renewed their most generous hospitality, and did all they possibly could for my benefit. My dear friend Miss Field came to meet me at Tjumen. I was glad to get under her care again; but, notwithstanding my friend's remonstrances, I started for Ekaterinburg the next day, feeling very anxious to move on towards St. Petersburg, where so much work awaited me.

At Ekaterinburg we were welcomed and entertained by Mrs. Thomas Yates, daughter of Mr. Wardroper; and we had to remain about a week, my bad health preventing me from continuing the journey at once.

When able to get about a little, I went, with Miss Field, to see the sisters at the convent there, in order to interest them in the lepers; and, before leaving, I gave them Testaments, which were most gratefully received. The following letter was sent to me by one of them :—

"HIGHLY-RESPECTED MISS KATE,

"From myself, and in the name of all our sisters, I send you our sincere gratitude for the attention you have bestowed upon us sinners. We do not know how, and we cannot find words, to express our feelings for you. We look upon you, not only by your social position, but especially by your spiritual life, as far above us, considering the great deed you have accomplished in visiting such unfortunate sufferers —a work which would hardly be undertaken by any one. Not one of us will ever forget your visit; and, as we daily read the precious words in the Holy Testaments we have received from you, we raise, and will continue to raise, heartfelt prayers to the Almighty Creator to prolong your precious life, to protect your health, and strengthen you to continue your great work; also praying that the Lord may uphold and ground in faith and patience those unfortunate, suffering lepers, and soon alleviate their condition.

"Wishing you good health and success in everything, we present our deep respect, and humbly beg, if it will not inconvenience you, to give our greetings to Anna Ivanovna Field.

"With sincere respect and devotion,

"I remain,

"Ever ready to serve you,

"CLAUDIA KALOUGINA,

"Nun of the Tichvinsky Convent.

"Ekaterinburg, November 27th, 1891."

We set off again in a sledge, with 25° of cold, towards Moscow, or, rather, Zlatoust; and this 300 versts of sledge-riding, with its accompaniments of filthy post-stations, dirty people, and swarming vermin, threatened to prove the "last straw." The little life left in me was kept from expiring by my friend's unceasing care and ever-watchful consideration. How thankful I was to God that my former steadfast companion was at my side again!

When we approached Zlatoust, and I saw the steam

from engines and the station in the distance, a curious fit of emotion took hold of me. I was almost like a child, full of glee and excitement at seeing for the first time a railway-engine. My feelings can be well understood. Sledge-jolting, tarantass-bumping, horse-riding, and voyaging in cargo-boats had now all come to an end, and the luxury of a railway-train was to be experienced once more.

But this luxury had to be taken piecemeal, for the distance of some 900 versts to Moscow was too long and fatiguing for me to cover at one sitting, in my generally shattered condition. So we stopped and rested at two or three places.

At Ufa we saw Bishop Dionysius again, by whom we were greeted with a warm welcome. At Samara Governor Sverbeff received us with every kindness He had rooms prepared for us at the hotel, sent in dinners to us, and was most anxious about our comfort and welfare. I heard that there had been some lepers here a fortnight before our arrival, and that they had returned to their villages. At my request, a special meeting of doctors was summoned to discuss the question of leprosy in the Government of Samara, and to grant, if possible, the petitions for help which had come from lepers in the north and the south. I begged the doctors, under the leadership of the governor, to gather the lepers into a separate place of shelter, and to collect funds for their relief; and this they promised to do as soon as the famine came to an end. Before leaving the town, I had the satisfaction of seeing the lepers brought back from the villages and placed in separate rooms, where, besides being isolated, they would receive proper attention. Their arrival created considerable commotion and opposition; but I trust that, by this time, the people have become fully alive to the fact that, to care for the poor creatures who have already been stricken is an important measure for preventing the spread of the disease, especially as one of them kept a village shop:

The Bishop of Samara showed great interest in the work, and kindly sent me a letter, which I here venture to reproduce:

"YOUR EXCELLENCY, GRACIOUS MADAM,

"It was with lively interest that I read the account of Your Excellency's wonderful journey.

"Deeply touched by the unfortunate suffering state of the Yakutsk lepers, whose relief is the object of your journey, I thank God, from the depth of my heart, that in you He has raised such a charitable servant, who does not stop before any difficulties, but, with thorough self-denial, goes forth to help the most unfortunate of mortals.

"Your work is a holy work. May the Lord crown it with full success.

"Enclosing herein my mite towards your good

work, I have the honour to remain, with deep respect,

> " Your Excellency's humble servant,

>> " VLADIMIR,

>> " Bishop of Samara and Stavropol.

" November 30th, 1891."

I arrived once more in Moscow in December, nearly eleven months since setting out on that eventful day, February 1st, 1891. I kept quiet and rested for three days, seeing none of my Russian friends but Madame Costanda, and then set off for St. Petersburg, where I hoped to establish the headquarters of a scientific society for investigating the state of lepers, and controlling measures for their relief wherever lepers existed throughout the Russian Empire. In this plan I received the support of Professor Peterson, of whom I shall have more to say in the next chapter.

CHAPTER XIV.

RESULTS AND PROSPECTS.

Audience with Her Imperial Majesty the Empress—Miss Florence Nightingale and the Countess Tolstoi—Assistance given by the Head Procurator—The publication of the narrative of my journey—Mr. Emory Smith, and the drawing-room meeting at his house—Address by Professor Peterson—Madame Strekaloff, and the Society of Ants—Visits to leper colonies at Riga and Dorpat—Plan and arrangements for the proposed colony in Yakutsk—The lepers to have the best of everything—Ways and means—Princess Shachovsky, and her community of sisters at Moscow—Five sisters volunteer to go to Yakutsk—Activity of the Society of Ants—Professor Pospeloff, and the medical meeting in Moscow—Letter of thanks—Princess Shachovsky, and her active support and kindness—THE NAME OF CHRIST—The wants of the suffering obliterating religious distinctions—Gift of His Imperial Highness the Czarevitch—Efficacy of prayer—Departure of the sisters for Yakutsk—A " Leper Sunday " appointed for a collection throughout the Empire—Future work—" The love of Christ constraineth us."

THE next four months I was busy, both in St. Petersburg and in Moscow, interesting the Russians, high and low, on behalf of the lepers.   This chapter will, therefore, contain the chief results of my journey to Siberia ; and without going into details, which might only weary the reader, I hope to present an outline of the

practical outcome, so far, of the mission I was con-
strained to undertake.

Her Imperial Majesty the Empress was indisposed
on my arrival in St. Petersburg; and my audience
with Her Majesty was therefore delayed for some time.
At last I was honoured with a long audience, which
was a private one; but I may be allowed to say that
Her Majesty took the most lively and tender interest
in the lepers, and promised to exert all Her Imperial
influence to help forward the work. Her Imperial
Majesty also headed the list of donors to the fund
which was shortly started.

Here I must speak of the Countess Tolstoi. Men
generally have their ideal hero, and women their ideal
of womanhood. It goes without saying that my ideal
of an almost perfect Englishwoman is Miss Florence
Nightingale; as the queen of nurses to suffering
humanity, she stands forth as the embodiment of what
a woman can and should be. Next to Miss Florence
Nightingale, the woman I love and reverence the most
is the Countess Alexandrine Tolstoi. As Miss Nightingale is my ideal in her sphere of life, so the Countess
Tolstoi is my ideal in hers. Holding a position of
immense power and influence, remarkable for her
wisdom and discretion, a clever linguist, a perfect lady
and a true Christian, one who knows not how to stoop
to any littleness in life, who possesses the very soul of
honour, the Countess Tolstoi is unique amongst women

who are placed by God in circumstances of serious responsibility and wide-extending influence. The Countess Tolstoi has been my mother in Russia in all the difficulties and trials I had to encounter; and if only the lepers may learn to love her for all the thought and help she has given them, one of my fervent desires will be fulfilled.

My interviews with His Excellency the Head Procurator of the Synod brought about results which exceeded my highest expectations. I gave him the written account, signed by the Russian official who accompanied me, of my visits to the lepers. This account was published, by the Procurator's instructions, in the *Church Intelligence*, a weekly paper circulated all over Russia. Not content with this notice, which would probably come under the eyes of nearly every reader in the Empire, the Procurator had the article re-printed in pamphlet form, with the title, "The Journey of an English Sister of Mercy into the Yakutsk Government to help the Lepers." He ordered 40,000 copies to be printed and to be spread throughout Russia, in order that the interest of all classes of people might be secured. The proceeds were to be devoted to the Leper Fund, to which the Procurator had contributed £300. I should also mention that the pamphlet contained a note to the effect that contributions might be sent for the lepers to the Synod.

The newspapers then took up the subject, and discussed it from various stand-points, thus giving further publicity to the wants of the lepers, and the measures proposed to relieve them.

The Medical Department kindly appointed Professor Peterson, a known student in leprosy, to assist me in the prosecution of my work. With his help a plan was drawn up for the projected colony, and a small meeting convened of doctors who had been to Yakutsk, and were well acquainted with the conditions and customs of both country and people. We all met, and thoroughly discussed the plan of the colony; the other doctors fully approved of Professor Peterson's and of my ideas in every detail of the building, etc.; thus the plan was definitely decided upon. The general arrangement of buildings was settled as follows :—

Ten separate houses for the lepers, each constructed for the accommodation of ten inmates; two hospitals (one for each sex) for patients in an advanced stage of the disease; a house for the doctor and his two assistants; a house for the sisters; a church, and a house for the priest; a building for workshops, also a bath-house, a bakehouse, and a mortuary. The sexes are to be kept apart, except in the case of a leper family; each house is to be provided with a garden, and space is left for a large kitchen garden to supply the wants of the whole of the colony. Each household is to have two cows, for which a proper stable will be provided.

In designing this plan, one object was steadfastly kept in view, namely, the happiness of the lepers. The small houses, rather than one or two large ones, favoured this object; for the lepers would be less likely to be perpetually conscious of their outcast condition and incurable malady, if divided into little households, than if brought together under one roof. And other endeavours will be made to give these poor doomed creatures bright and pleasant surroundings, so as to relieve their minds, as far as foresight and consideration can suggest, of any morbid and distressing consciousness that their life is only a " living death."

Material and workmanship are to be of the very best quality procurable ; and no pains will be spared to give the most miserable of God's creatures the best things that can in any way add to their comfort and happiness. I want this colony to be, in every sense, a model one ; and, with God's help, it *shall* be.

Having got the plans, and having formed an idea of the mode of working, the next thing was to find ways and means to build and support the colony. I hoped that in course of time the colony would, in some degree, support itself from the produce of the soil, and from other sources; but, after allowing a margin in this direction, I found it was quite necessary to raise £9000 for the buildings alone, exclusive of furniture, clothing, outfit, and maintenance.

I was introduced to **Mr. Emory Smith**, the United

States Minister at St. Petersburg. This gentleman took a very warm interest in the work, and not only favoured me with several interviews, but also made inquiries from Countess Tolstoi and others. A drawing-room meeting was afterwards held in his house, which was attended by twelve ladies-in-waiting of Her Imperial Majesty the Empress, and by many other leading ladies of the aristocracy. At the last moment I feared that, owing to my ill health, I should be unable to deliver the address that was expected from me. I managed, however, to give an outline of what had been done, and of the proposals for the benefit of the lepers. Professor Peterson, a true friend of the lepers, and the second best authority on leprosy in Russia, gave an address, and submitted a plan of the projected colony; and Mr. Souponeff, a Russian nobleman, and formerly a provincial governor, made a touching statement about the condition of the lepers in Yakutsk.

A letter of introduction was then sent me to a Moscow lady—Madame Strekaloff—who, later on, proved a most devoted friend to the lepers. Her name is loved and respected all over Moscow. She has been the founder of several philanthropic institutions, as well as founder and president of the Society for the Spread of Useful Books; although advanced in age, she works incessantly for the benefit of others, and enters readily into any new good work, as my readers will see by the work she did for the lepers. She asked me at once to come to

Moscow, and re-arouse the interest of that great philanthropic centre.

But before going to Moscow, I made arrangements to visit the lepers in the Baltic provinces. Professor Peterson, who, as I have already mentioned, had been appointed to help me in carrying out all my plans, accompanied me on this journey.

At Riga I found quite a charming little leper colony, which emanated from a philanthropic society, due to the earnest work of Dr. Bergmann, another friend to the lepers, and which had been designed and constructed on the newest and best sanitary principles. Although containing accommodation for forty lepers, there were only twenty-two inmates as yet, though I was told that Riga contained sixty other lepers still scattered in the town; some of these I visited myself. There was a large room, with a harmonium, and other means of recreation for the patients, an operating room, a mortuary, and other small buildings, forming altogether a little colony. Dr. Bergmann, with several other competent assistants, has charge of the place.

There were eighteen lepers at the Dorpat hospital, which is another comfortable little building. A second hospital is now being built with funds raised by a society. Professor de Wahl was the founder of this society; his memory is cherished and loved, not only by the town of Dorpat, but by the numbers of students now scattered in different parts of the Empire, as well as in other countries, who had studied under him ; and the prayers of the lepers he has so wonderfully helped will form an ever-living memorial.   Professor Dehio is now continuing the work of his loved and able teacher.

These visits to Riga and Dorpat proved helpful, also, in obtaining the approval of the above-mentioned authorities in leprosy to our plan of the Siberian colony, which they unanimously admired.

After much anxious deliberation and prayer I decided to adopt Madame Strekaloff's suggestion, and to try what could be done to raise funds in Moscow, in spite of the expense of the journey.   But before setting out, I heard a piece of good news which cheered and encouraged me.   A Moscow friend, Princess Gagarine, informed me that, owing to the wide circulation of the pamphlet containing the account of my journey, the condition of the lepers had come to the ears of a community of sisters of mercy in Moscow, of which the devoted Princess Shachovskoy was the head.   Both the princess and the sisters had become deeply interested in the story of the lepers' sufferings, and one of the sisters at once begged the princess to allow her to go and nurse the poor creatures.   It seems that for two years she had been praying that God would give her an opportunity of devoting her life to leper work.   As soon as she had laid her petition before the princess, four other sisters followed her example.   How deep was my thankfulness to God that He had put it into the heart of these women to take up the cross and follow the Master!

On reaching Moscow I found that Madame Strekaloff had most thoroughly grasped the condition and wants of the lepers. The Society of Ants, consisting of Russian ladies engaged in benevolent and philanthropic work, of which she was the head, entered with true Russian enthusiasm into all the proposals, and formed a committee with the special object of providing clothing for one hundred lepers, furniture for the colony, and the linen required for all purposes.

The next movement was amongst the Moscow newspapers; the work was discussed in no half-hearted manner, and important contributions followed, all this money being sent to the proper official fund. Then the medical men became interested, led by Professor Pospeloff, Director of the Moscow Great Miasnitsky Hospital, and President of the Moscow Dermatological and Venerological Society. At one of the committee meetings of the "Ants," the professor spoke in a most sympathetic way about the lepers, and asked me to give a report of my investigation at a special meeting which he wished to convene in the hall of the Miasnitsky Hospital. The hall was crowded by the medical staff, and representatives of the leading Moscow societies. The five sisters who had volunteered to go to Yakutsk also attended, and were introduced to the

President. After my report had been read by the President, he gave the following address :—

"GENTLEMEN MEMBERS OF THE SOCIETY,

"We have just heard Miss Marsden's interesting report. Thanks to it, we are now acquainted with the unsanitary condition in which the greater part of the Yakutsk lepers live, and which, without a doubt, needs a radical reorganisation in the interests both of the lepers themselves, and of those in perfect health surrounding them.

"On the authority of the documents presented by Miss Marsden to our Society, we see that the local doctors and administration of the Yakutsk province have for some time past been filled with an earnest desire of organising a better care of the lepers of that province ; but, unfortunately, all these desires and the appointments connected with them have up to this time been made only on paper—that is to say, during the space of sixty-five years.

"Again, on the authority of these documents, which have been looked through by myself, together with the following members of our Society—Doctors N. P. Fiveisky, N. S. Speransky, and L. N. Moursine—we could not but help coming to the conclusion that the question of the abnormal condition of the Yakut lepers is far from a new one, and arose, as I already said, in 1827 by the initiative of Dr. Ouklonsky ; but since then,

and up to the present time, it has remained in the same
state—that is to say, during the last sixty-five years.

"In the meantime, leprosy has existed in the
Yakutsk province, and has been spreading among the
Yakuts up to this time, undoubtedly demanding
energetic and sanitary measures to be taken, similar
to those long in practice in Norway, and, at present,
also in our own Baltic provinces. These measures
chiefly consist in the isolation of lepers; and the in-
vestigations made in Bergen, in Norway, have shown
that it is only by the isolation of lepers, in special
sanitary colonies, that a steady decrease in the number
of lepers can be effected, and, consequently, the total
disappearance of the disease.

"Thanks to energetic, self-denying, and tender-
hearted Miss Marsden, the question of caring for the
lepers of the Yakutsk province has now received an
immense impetus towards its accomplishment. At the
present time the Government has already given directions about the organisation of a colony in accordance
with contemporary medical opinion, similar to the
colony built near Riga. Miss Marsden has already
collected over 25,000 roubles, which she has remitted
into due hands, and we cannot but feel exceedingly
grateful to Miss Marsden for such a beginning.

"In giving Miss Marsden our due tribute of gratitude
for all she has gone through in behalf of the lepers,
her self-denial, her energy, etc., I must say a few

words about Miss Marsden herself, who, as much as she is energetic, is modest in the valuation of her work. I want to say a few words about those difficulties and that risk which Miss Marsden experienced in her journey in Siberia. It is not by any personal impression, or on the grounds of any conversation that I may have had with Miss Marsden about her journey, but on the authority of the official documents I hold, that I have come to the conclusion that Miss Marsden's journey was a very dangerous one, and risky, in the sense of the possibility of the contagion of leprosy. Indeed, for a woman to accomplish ninety versts a day on horseback, riding in all about 3000 versts, is an immense feat, which undoubtedly has cost the traveller her health.

"The ispravnick of the Viluisk Circuit, Antonovitch, who is well acquainted with the local conditions of the place, in his report of the 31st July, 1891, states that, to reach the lepers on horseback, he was obliged to direct very energetic work to be done in clearing a road along the Viluisk Circuit in the Tayga for the length of 1500 versts, where, according to his words, there would have been no possibility to pass in the summer; but, notwithstanding the clearing of the said road, the ispravnick in the same report speaks of Miss Marsden's journey as terrible and difficult.* How far this journey

---

* " Ispravnick of the Viluisk Circuit of the Kobaisky Nassleg Sredni Viluisk Oulousse," July 31st, 1891.

along the Tayga was indeed difficult, even on horseback, and often quite impossible, we can judge from
what is said in the report of the medical inspector, Dr.
Smirnoff, who, when he was visiting the village of
Lioutchinsk, which was thirty versts from the administration, was obliged to send for the lepers, as there was
no possibility to get up to their dwelling-place. The
intense heat during the day, the cold at night, the
constant assault of mosquitoes, the dampness from the
marshes, all this made the journey anything but easy,
and it has truly been described by the Feldsher
Paramonoff, who accompanied Miss Marsden to the
lepers. 'Looking at you, a woman,' says he, in his
letter, 'bearing this difficult journey with so much
courage, and the sleepless nights after which you could
hardly keep on the saddle, and yet, for the sake of the
work, travelling ninety versts a day, to us men,
accustomed to all inconveniences, your energy and
Christian self-denial were almost incredible.' Mr.
Paramonoff adds that after the labours of the day, when
resting, they had often to share their scanty morsel,
which clearly showed that, besides all the other inconveniences, they had to suffer from lack of sufficient
food.

"Miss Marsden's journey to Yakutsk will bring
undoubted help to the lepers of Yakutsk, similar to
that occasioned by the journey to the lepers in the
south of Russia of the well-known student in leprosy,

Professor Munch, which roused interest in the lepers of that part; of Dr. Peterson, in St. Petersburg, and Professors Wahl, Bergmann, and others in the Baltic provinces. Miss Marsden's journey has certainly brought practical help. Therefore, gentlemen, allow me to thank Miss Marden in the name of our Society for her interesting information, and for the hard work and travelling that she has accomplished in behalf of the lepers, herself probably running the risk of catching leprosy."

The President then moved a vote of thanks, seconded by Professor Mansouroff, which it has been thought desirable to give verbatim.

"DEAR MADAM,

"Having heard your most interesting report about the insanitary condition of the lepers of the Sredni Viluisk Circuit of the Yakutsk province, the Moscow Venerological and Dermatological Society begs you to accept the expression of their most sincere gratitude, not only for the information that you have kindly given, but also for the official documents which you have kindly presented to our Society for their inspection.

"On the authority of these documents, as well as on that of the report we have just heard about the deplorable unsanitary conditions of the lepers, which you have yourself witnessed when visiting them, our Society fully endorses your idea about the urgent necessity of properly caring for these unfortunate patients; at the same time it believes that it is indispensable to do this, not only out of feelings of philanthropy, but for the protection of the healthy from contagion, which inevitably takes place in the non-sanitary surroundings in which, according to the reports of the local doctors and your own, the lepers live.

" Having undertaken this journey to the lepers, far from easy, especially for a woman, setting aside the possibility of yourself getting the disease among these sufferers, you have got acquainted with their position on the spot. You have not limited yourself to making a collection of documents for a tourist's memorial, as is generally done, but, with true-hearted solicitude of a sister of mercy, you have roused a feeling of sympathy in our Society for these unfortunate sufferers which has called forth a flow of contributions for the organisation of a sanitary colony for them, which all the other lepers scattered in the different corners of Russia may indeed envy.

" In rendering you our due tribute of respect for your energy, self-denial, and heartfelt solicitude on behalf of the lepers, our Society once again thanks you for the labours you have gone through to help the lepers, and sincerely wishes you further success in your heavy and dangerous, though exceedingly sympathetic and philanthropic, task.

"President of the Society, A. POSPELOFF.

(The Stamp of the Society).

"The Moscow Venerological and Dermatological Society.

"Secretary of the Society, N. FEVEISKY."

ADDRESS DELIVERED BY THE VICE-PRESIDENT OF THE MOSCOW VENEROLOGICAL AND DERMATOLOGICAL SOCIETY, PROFESSOR N. P. MANSOUROFF, AT THE MEETING OF THE SOCIETY, APRIL 22ND, 1892, WITH REFERENCE TO THE REPORT MADE BY MISS KATE MARSDEN, SISTER OF MERCY, ABOUT THE SANITARY CONDITION OF THE LEPERS OF THE VILUISK CIRCUIT OF THE YAKUTSK PROVINCE.

"MUCH-RESPECTED MISS,

"When a tourist undertakes a long journey, it is certainly to satisfy his own curiosity; but when a woman decides to visit a distant country, thousands of miles away from her own land, with the sole purpose of getting to know the position of sufferers, victims of the most terrible of diseases, leprosy; when she willingly submits to all the inconveniences of the journey—to the severe cold of an almost savage country, to hunger and to fatigue, her only recompense being the hope of alleviating the sufferings of these unfortunate people, and evoking a feeling of sympathy for them in the civilised world—then not only does the journey of such a woman merit the sympathies of scientists and philanthropists, but the person herself inspires their respect and their admiration.

"Allow me then, Miss, to express to you my sentiments of respect and sympathy for the idea that you have so honourably carried out, the contributions that you have called forth, which will create a shelter and hospital for these poor sufferers. Accept my gratitude for the information you have kindly given us. The Society of Dermatology, of which I have the honour to be Vice-President, shares my sentiments for your noble mission."

The Princess Shachovskoy, whose deep sympathy had been aroused, had called to see me with the five sisters. And here let me draw attention to the wrong ideas sometimes fostered respecting the nursing sisters of the orthodox Greek Church.

It is far from my wish to draw any comparisons or contrasts, but I am bound, in simple justice, to bear emphatic testimony to the spontaneous sympathy accorded to my work by members of the Greek Church wherever I went in Russia, in spite of their knowledge of the fact that I was a foreigner and a Protestant. The fact of my being a Protestant was no bar to a ready and patient hearing of my appeal. The vast differences in point of faith and doctrine that separated me from them roused no prejudice ; for did I not appeal to them in the NAME OF CHRIST, and on behalf of His lepers ? The name of Christ is all-powerful everywhere, and obliterates the important distinctions of doctrine and practice where the crying needs of suffering humanity are concerned. Religious prejudices and national prejudices were all forgotten, when from the north there came the piteous wail from naked, starving, deformed, and crippled lepers, " Come over and help us ! "

Another fact also occurs to my mind with pathetic force as I write—and I mention it with all humility and thankfulness. I know that to-day, in many a dwelling in Russia, both amongst rich and poor, prayers arise on my behalf to the Great Father of us all. And I, a Protestant, and an unworthy, halting follower of Christ, lift up my voice to the Great Unseen for blessings to descend upon the millions of Russia.

The prompt way in which the Princess Shachovskoy answered my appeal was only one instance out of many where a call from Christ leads men and women of the Greek Church to forget everything but their duty to obey. The institution over which the princess presides contains about 400 inmates, afflicted with various diseases, and many of them insane. The work of nursing is carried on by sixty sisters, and the institution is entirely supported by the princess's efforts.

In conversation with the princess she said, with

reference to the sisters who had volunteered, and the work in Yakutsk: "When I took my vow to follow Christ, I did not take it to follow my own will; and if I were only younger I would gladly go myself; indeed, I have to stifle almost envious thoughts when recollecting that the sisters are going."

Portraits of the princess and three of the sisters are given in the accompanying illustration—the other two sisters, being absent, could not be photographed at the time; and few readers can fail to discern in the beautiful face of the aged princess the reflection of her devotion and love to humanity.

The sisters, having proffered their services, the question arose as to the cost of their outfit, their travelling expenses, and their means of living. For the sake of giving the lepers immediate nursing attention, and preparing them for reception into the colony, it was proposed to send off some sisters without delay. It was thought desirable that I should return to St. Petersburg in order to find the money to meet these expenses. The princess very kindly went with me. I was far from well, and the dear princess herself tended me, and went out to fetch my food, buying all kinds of fruit, which I was much in need of, and of which I had been deprived, together with vegetables, almost throughout my journey to and from Siberia.

Soon after reaching the capital I wrote to his Imperial Highness the Czarevitch, as President of a

Committee for the Relief of the Starving, asking for the money required for the sisters' expenses. Most prompt and kind was the reply. In two days His Imperial Highness sent a contribution of £500 from his private purse to cover these expenses.

The letter which His Imperial Highness ordered to be written to me was as follows:—

"MADAM,

"I have the honour to inform you, that I had the joy of submitting to His Imperial Highness, my Lord the Grand Duke Cezarevitch, your petition concerning the help you purpose rendering to the unfortunate lepers of the Yakutsk Government; and that His Imperial Highness, taking a lively interest in the good work undertaken by your generous devotion, has deigned to entrust me to remit to you, for the said cause, the sum of 5,000 roubles from His Highness.

"Fulfilling the wish of my Lord the Grand Duke Cezarevitch, I have the honour to send you, with the present letter, the 5,000 roubles stated, begging you, Madam, to accept the assurance of my perfect esteem and highest consideration,

"V. PLEVE.

"St. Petersbourg, April 29th, 1892."

In a few days this contribution was followed by an anonymous gift of £100.

I regarded these gifts, and all the help that had been

proffered, as distinct answers to prayers. Some kind-hearted people who read this book may perhaps assign all the results named to natural causes; but from childhood upwards I have ever possessed a deep conviction concerning the efficacy of prayer, and I trace a great many events in my life and in connection with my work, not to human instrumentality, but to the direct guidance and help of God in answer to prayer.

With regard to a party of working nuns going to Yakutsk to attend to the manual labour of the colony, the Head Procurator granted his permission for this departure from monastic regulations. The five nursing sisters from the institution of the princess left Moscow in May last, and by this time I trust they are in the midst of the leper district, ministering to the wants of these poor creatures. The departure of the sisters for Yakutsk was notified to me in the following letter :—

Letter from the Princess Shachovskoy of Moscow.

" My dearly-loved Sister,

" Yesterday, May 17 (29), having announced in the papers the definite departure of the sisters, on arriving at the station with my dear travellers, I saw a man of venerable appearance approaching me, who asked me to accept 51 roubles (£5 2s. 0d.) for the travelling expenses of the sisters. Another gave me 100 roubles (£10), a third 200 roubles (£20), half for the sisters and half for the poor unfortunate lepers.

Again, a fourth brought 25 roubles (£2 10s. 0d.). Very touching prayers were offered by an earnest pastor, a great number of people being present, all surrounding the sisters, and, with tears, wishing them a happy journey. It was indeed a solemn hour. Why could not our good angel, our beloved Kate Marsden, have been present at this beautiful religious service, which would indeed have filled her heart with joy? Madame Costanda will, no doubt, also send you details about the sisters' departure. When the moment for saying farewell had come, as the head of the sisters took leave of her aged mother of seventy-five, her family, and her country, no one present could remain indifferent at the sight of these good-byes, which were heartrending on the part of the mother, but calm and sad on the part of the daughter, who for the last three years had been waiting for the accomplishment of her earnest desire to consecrate herself to the care of the lepers. When at last the third bell put an end to the heartrending scene, and after having watched the train out of sight, which perhaps was carrying off five victims of devoted love, I went straight to the telegraph office to send you the telegram with the news of their departure, which will certainly gladden your heart.

"Yours for ever,

"NATALIE."

But, what I may call, the crowning result of my efforts remains yet to be named. I understood that on the Sunday when the Gospel of the Blind was appointed to be read, a collection was made in the churches throughout Russia on behalf of the blind, and that this collection amounted annually to over £4000. I went to the Head Procurator, and, in the name of Christ, I begged that a collection might be made for the lepers on the Sunday when the Gospel of the Leper is appointed to be read, and, to my joy, the request was granted; and on the 13th of next December the first collection, I hope, will be made in aid of lepers throughout the Empire. I cannot adequately express my gratitude to the Head Procurator for so willingly granting this boon, and all the requests with regard to the lepers which were presented to him.

I have no complete return yet of the amount collected in Russia, and of the proceeds of the various publications; but whatever amount may be lacking, I hope to make up from the profits of this book and of my lecturing tour in America. From these latter sources I am anticipating that there will be a sufficient return to carry out my plans amongst the lepers of Siberia, and also for the purpose of helping lepers and leper societies throughout the world, irrespective of nationality and creed.

Since returning to England last spring, I have been busily occupied in gathering strength for the work before me, and in preparing this book, which I devoutly trust will be accepted both in England, America, and other countries, not as a record of vainglorious effort, but as an earnest endeavour to arouse sympathy on behalf of the most miserable members of the human race.

In bidding farewell to my readers, I earnestly and humbly ask for their prayers that I may be guided and supported in the work to which, by God's grace, I have been led to dedicate a feeble and faulty life; and the best prayer that I can offer on behalf of you, dear readers, is that Christ may ever dwell in you, and you in Him, that you may thus be ever bound up with His life, and bound to the heart of suffering humanity, responsive to every throb of pain, and eager to relieve the children of sorrow.

The "claims of humanity" are insufficient, alone, to sustain prolonged consecration to the service of the suffering: a higher inspiration is required. A gentleman once visited a hospital where the victims of a terrible malady were sheltered. After passing through the wards, and noting the heartrending and almost repulsive condition of the patients, he said to the nurse who accompanied him, "You must have a great deal of the 'enthusiasm of humanity' to keep you in such a place as this."

"Enthusiasm of humanity, sir," the nurse replied, "*that* motive would not keep us here for a single day—the 'LOVE OF CHRIST CONSTRAINETH US.'"

APPENDIX.

I.

Testimonial from Her Highness, Countess Tolstoi, Lady of Honour to Her Imperial Majesty the Empress of Russia.

It is by my own initiative, and with the desire of testifying to a touching truth, that I give this writing to Miss Kate Marsden, feeling sure that every Russian would be ready to do the same.

The work Miss Kate Marsden has undertaken in our country is so important, so full of humanitarian charity, that we cannot fail to see in Miss Marsden an instrument chosen by the Lord Himself to alleviate the condition— moral as well as physical—of the poor lepers. Upheld by God, and by her great faith in Him, Miss Marsden has in a very short time laid the first foundation of a colony, destined to create a new existence for these miserable outcasts. Her love for them never wavered before any obstacle, and this same love has kindled many hearts which have been united by her generous idea.

Our august Sovereign herself has deigned to give Miss Marsden proofs of her sympathy, receiving her several times; and, being deeply touched by her Christian devotion, she had the kindness to grant her her protection, and to help her to accomplish her journey in Siberia. We will have the possibility of reading the stirring details some day.

The immense difficulties Miss Marsden has overcome have only deepened her zeal for her cause, for which she would willingly give her life, as she has already given her health. May all generous souls who know how to appreciate such sacrifices unite with us in asking God to bless this work and the one who has consecrated herself to it.

Countess A. Tolstoi,
Lady of Honour to Her Majesty
the Empress of Russia.

Winter Palace, St. Petersburg, May 13, 1892.

II.

Testimonial.

Deeply-respected and Christ-loving Miss Marsden,

The fatal hour of separation has come. It is a sore trial for me to bid you farewell. You have animated

us, and have roused in us a deep feeling of love for our
suffering ones, which up to now had only existed for us
in the traditions connected with our Lord and Saviour
Jesus Christ. Your courage, notwithstanding all the
threats, when starting for Siberia into the depths of a
distant country to help the lepers; your work there
among people whose language even was unknown to
you; your self-denial to alleviate the condition of these
forgotten sufferers for so many years—all this has greatly
endeared you to me; and I pray the Almighty to
strengthen and protect your precious life so that you may
see the realisation of the colony in Viluisk of the Yakutsk
Government, which, as a bright angel, you planned and
prayed for. Rest assured that your work will not remain
unfruitful in truly philanthropic Moscow, and as well as
in our Society of Ants, which has been roused by your
incessant work in behalf of these perishing people, and
especially as it has at its head Madame Strekaloff, a true
Christian angel of mercy, as well as warm Christian
members, who have so much sympathy for you and for
your sufferers the lepers. We will put all our efforts
forth to accomplish all your good desires. We will pray
that our Heavenly Father, for the sake of His crucified
Son our Saviour, may bring this holy and truly godly
work to a full and happy issue.

May the Lord protect you.

With deep respect and warm love,

Yours,

AGATHA COSTANDA,
Wife of the Commander of all the
troops in MOSCOW.

MOSCOW, May, 1892.

III.

Letter from Father John Vinokouroff.

DEEPLY RESPECTED SISTER OF MERCY,

I take the liberty of expressing my sincere and true gratitude for your affable attention and good-will towards me. I cannot find words tender enough to thank you for your remembrance of so miserable a sinner as myself, so kindly expressed in your letter, written from Irkutsk the 20th September, and also for your photograph.

My wife and daughter, as well as myself, were so overjoyed at receiving your photograph that we were quite beside ourselves. We did nothing but kiss it and shed tears of joy. Our prayers for your precious health will constantly go up to the Almighty Creator; and when we are called away from this world, even then will we pray to the Saviour for you. As soon as I got your letter, I went to the lepers living near the administration, and I also went to the one living alone—the one we met on our way along the side of the river. I translated literally into Yakut all that you kindly wrote to them and to me; and I also read it to all the Yakuts of Sredni Viluisk I met on my way, as well as to those in the administration. They all listened to your information with prayers and tears of joy, and kissed your photograph, which I had taken with me, at the same time making the sign of the Cross, and prostrating themselves to the ground; in fact, there was no end to our joy, on receipt of your letter.

But the delight of the poor lepers—my spiritual children—was indescribable. How can we help being joyful and crying for joy when we think of what God has sent us—a deliverer for our poor unfortunate lepers!

All those that heard from me about your letter—about the trouble and work you were doing, and of all that you had kindly sent the unfortunate lepers—all the Yakuts, as well as the lepers themselves, begged of me to lay at your feet their most sincere gratitude. My wife, daughter, and myself, also, lay at your feet our most sincere gratitude, wishing you every good thing in this life, but specially good health—this precious gift of God, so necessary for the continuation of the good work you have begun for my unfortunate spiritual children, the lepers, who are so constantly in your heart and mind. Your letter I had the pleasure of translating into Yakutsk, both for the Golova and the lepers.

The day after I received your letter I had a service of prayer, for your precious health, in the house of Nicholas Markovitch. All those that accompanied you from Viluisk were present.

I remain,

The humble servant and constant prayer-offerer for the merciful worker, on behalf of the unfortunate lepers,

PRIEST JOHN VINOKOUROFF.

November 4th, 1891.

IV.

Extract from Father Vinokouroff's Report on the Condition of the Lepers.

LEPROSY OF SREDNI VILUISK.

Since 1879, when I was appointed to serve in the Sredni Viluisk Oulousse, I have had to mix among the lepers living in my parish. When I first came there I used to visit the Viluisk town hospital, which had been organised two or three years before my arrival. After I came there the lepers remained two or three years longer in the hospital, and then by somebody's order—I do not know by whose—they were sent altogether back into the oulousse, to their different nasslegs. Not one of the lepers who entered the hospital was cured, and five of the number died and were buried by me. I also used to visit the leper hospital during Lent, to help the lepers perform their devotions and to administer the Holy Sacrament. The life of the lepers in the hospital was very good under all conditions—first, because every day they saw healthy people; they could talk with the Yakut keepers of the hospital, from whom they could always get some information about the town; secondly, they were in warm rooms, and were fed with better and more nourishing food; thirdly, they used every day to see the Russian feldsher, who gave them some medical help, though the said help was utterly useless. . . .

As soon as a Yakut recognises a leper amongst them —be it father, mother, brother, sister, son, or daughter— immediately he is thrust out from the family for ever, and never has any further connection with them during the whole of his life. He is sent 10 or 20 versts away from his home, where he has to remain to the end of his life alone, unless there happens to be some other unfortunate leper sent from the community to share his miserable fate. . . .

When there are only one or two lepers together, and they do not appear at the appointed time to fetch their food, then the whole of the community of the nassleg assemble and choose the bravest among them, who is hired for a sum of money, collected from the whole of the community, to go to the lepers and see whether they are dead or not, or perhaps have got to the condition of being unable to move about. They try and place several lepers together, and in the case of those that are in a very advanced state of disease, the others that are in a better state can help them, and in case of death the lepers who are in a better condition can bury those who die.

On the whole of the earth you will not find men in so miserable a condition as the Sredni Viluisk lepers. The name leper is used by the Russian tchinovnicks who are sent for service into the Viluisk Circuit as a swear word. In fact, the whole of the Sredni Viluisk Oulousse is considered so bad a place that it is called the leper place.

Although besides the Sredni Viluisk Oulousse there are other lepers to be found in other oulousses, these latter lepers hide from the authorities, and therefore are not known. . . .

During the time of my twelve years' service we had epidemics of small-pox, measles, scarlet fever, and virulent quinsy. During the time of these epidemics all my efforts to convince them that it was necessary to isolate those patients only resulted in the answer that, as it was not leprosy, they did not see the need of doing it. Why trouble? All would not die; but only those appointed to do so by God. They used to say that all these diseases were sent by God, but leprosy was sent by the devil.

This paper was received by me from the Priest, Father John Vinokouroff, of the Lioutchinsky parish of the Sredni Viluisk Oulousse, living in the town of Viluisk, of the Yakutsk Government, to remit to Miss Kate Marsden. I received the paper June 17th, 1891, in the Sredni Viluisk native administration.

(Signed) PÉTROFF,
Tchinovnick for special service to the
Yakutsk Governor.

V.

An expression of deep gratitude from Gregory Eremeieff, Golova, or Chief, of the Sredni Viluisk District.

To Miss Kate Marsden.

Being the Golova, or chief, of this oulousse I escorted you throughout it, visiting all the haunts of my leper people, and I now have the honour to present to you, dear Madam, from myself and from the whole of my tribe (oulousse), the expression of our great and heartfelt thanks for your charitable and brave undertaking in going through most impassable parts of my oulousse, so as to visit and help my poor lepers. Also, if I may express my earnest desire framed in this request, I beg that, if possible, you will lay at the feet of Her Imperial Majesty the Empress the expression of our loyal and devoted love and gratitude for Her Imperial Majesty's immediate protection of our unfortunate lepers.

Consequently, using simple expressions, being an uneducated man, and much troubled by the sufferings of these unfortunate people, I must say I find your great journey similar to that when our Saviour Jesus Christ, who was born on earth years ago, and having to bear all kinds of trials, saved the human race; and thus, while making the sign of the Cross, our hearts full, we glance up to heaven, saying the sun has risen, full of bright mercy and joy over us and our unfortunate sick people. O Lord, what a kind and merciful deliverance of such unfortunate people! He is working for us through you. It is all so precious to us; and what a recompense you will have from the King of Heaven and of earth for such charity and liberality! For our own sakes, Lord, protect this good lady, and all her fellow-travellers, so that she may reach her own country well and happy.

(Signed)   GREGORY YAKOVLEFF EREMEIEFF,
Golova (chief of the tribe).

VI.

Letter from V. Paramonoff, doctor's assistant, who went with me from Viluisk to visit the lepers.

MISS MARSDEN.

DEAR MADAM,

It was with heartfelt joy that I received the news of your safe arrival in Irkutsk, and I pray that God may give you strength to fulfil to the end the gracious and high commission of our kind mother, Her Majesty the Empress.

From this time the unfortunate suffering lepers—cast away from all people, whose dreadful position, God forbid that anyone should even have a sight of—have a loving mother in their Supreme Empress, and a sister in you, who has consecrated all her strength and life to alleviate as much as possible their truly bitter existence.

Thank God that He has given me an opportunity of being of some little help in this holy work.

As a citizen and Christian, I am bound to express my sincere gratitude for the hearty interest and self-sacrifice, which it is not possible to describe, but which, as your constant fellow-traveller, I saw in every step of your difficult and dangerous journey, full of every possible privation.

Your truly highly Christian manner with the patients, your tears which you tried to conceal from us, and only gave them free course when hidden behind some leper hut, but which you could not quite hide from those who

were watching your every step so as to protect you, and
enable you to fulfil the sacred will of Her Majesty the
Empress, whose heart was in each word of comfort you
spoke to the unfortunate sufferers; your more than hearty
manner to the natives, and your help in their needs, and,
at last, your manner with all your fellow-travellers, myself in the number, cannot be remembered otherwise than
with sincere pleasure. No need to thank me; it was no
trouble to carry out your instructions with regard to the
lepers, but a high moral enjoyment, for your energy and
warmth of heart permeated us all. As we looked at you—
a woman so courageous, bearing the difficult journey and
sleepless nights, after which you could hardly keep in
your saddle, and yet for the work's sake doing 90 versts
a day—your energy and Christian self-denial seemed to us,
who were accustomed to hardships, incredible; and your
warm friendly manner in the tayga (vast marshy forest),
under the open sky, by the light of a flaming wood-pile,
when, after the labour of the day, we used to share our
scanty morsel, and the general interest in the work—all
this has drawn us closer together, so that I confess it was
hard to say good-bye to you in Yakutsk.

Accept the assurance of the deep respect and devotion
of your humble servant,

V. PARAMONOFF.

Viluisk, Yakutsk Government,
November 4th, 1891.

VII.

Letters from Lepers.

OUR LOVING PATRONESS MISS MARSDEN,

We thank you very much for the great gifts you
have sent us, which we have only just received. We will

always pray to God for you. We are still living in the same way as when you visited us. The frightful disease is torturing us in our miserable little huts; and we are suffering from cold and, in addition, from hunger. Only God alone knows and sees our wretched life. Last summer the crops failed; so that now the community cannot even give us one pound of flour, and we have not even a proper kettle to boil our tea in. Lord, protect our benefactress, Miss Marsden, like the apple of Thine eye.

OUR KIND AND PHILANTHROPIC MISS KATE MARSDEN,

This day we have had the happiness to receive your holy gifts, and also your letter, for which we have given a receipt. We thank you from the depths of our hearts. The Lord Jesus Christ will grant you heavenly and earthly happiness. We have to inform you that we live in a sad condition, suffering from cold and hunger in addition to our terrible disease. You yourself have witnessed our unfortunate existence. Our hope is in God, and in you for charitable help. We are constantly praying to God for your health and long life. May the Lord God bless you. After your visit one of our number died.

THE LEPERS OF LOUTCHINSKY AND TOGOUISKY
NASSLEG OF THE SREDNI VILUISK OULOUSSE.

Monday, February 24th, 1892.

The above letters were written at their request and dictation, and translated into the Russian language by me—Yakut, Government writer, Vasilliy Nikolaeff Novine.

VIII.

Protocol No. 3, of the Yakutsk Provincial Committee for public health; sitting of the 8th February, 1890, concerning the preventive measures to be taken for leprosy.

Were present:—President, the Governor V. L. Kolenko, Members of the Committee, the Vice-Governor P. P. Ostashkin, the chief Councillor of the Provincial Administration, K. C. Finistoff, Medical Inspector M. M. Smirnoff, the Provincial Veterinary Surgeon S. Y. Dmitrieff, the Police Master V. V. Souchatcheff, the Yakutsk Ispravnick E. D. Klimovsky, the Collegiate Councillor V. G. Gollmann.

The Governor, whilst inspecting the Viluisk Circuit, was convinced of the necessity of taking definite measures for leprosy, which is spreading more and more in the Viluisk Circuit, threatening, by its further development, to become a national calamity. In consequence of this, he finds it absolutely necessary to bring the question of preventive measures for leprosy before the Committee for Public Health, for their deliberation. From the report of the tchinovnick for special services, Collegiate Secretary P. Schachourdine, who had been specially sent into the Viluisk Circuit by the Governor of the Province, we learn that, in the Sredni Viluisk Oulousse of the Viluisk Circuit, a frightful disease has existed from olden times, called leprosy, and it has been acknowledged by law (c. xiii.) to be exceedingly contagious. The natives who fall victims to this dreadful disease are provided with food, sometimes with cattle, and are sent into the depths of the forest under strict command never to appear in the dwellings of the healthy Yakuts, and in general to keep away. Food is provided for these patients from the village to which they belong, and this food is brought to a certain spot in the forest, known to the lepers, generally in a sufficient quantity so as to prevent the latter coming for the food in case of insufficiency.

About ten years ago two hospitals were opened, one at a place called Latchima, in the Sredni Viluisk Oulousse, and the other in the town of Viluisk. The first of these hospitals was under the direction of Dr. Krasnoff and the medical assistant Antonovitch; the second under Dr. Bergmann. Both hospitals were especially for leper patients. But these hospitals, having given no satisfactory results, were closed.

The symptoms of leprosy are the following:—On the patient's face and cheeks a very noticeable red colour appears, the eyes get dull, and a special thoughtfulness is noticed in the eyes. The eye-brows and eye-lashes fall off, and gradually the whole organism of the patient becomes disfigured, and finally decays. The leper, according to the reports of the natives, can live twenty years and more. The natives who have fallen victims to this disease generally live near lakes in the depths of the forest in yourtas (little Yakut huts). The interior of these yourtas is not known to Mr. Schachourdine, as, however much he wanted to get acquainted with the interior of the said huts, he could not get into them on account of the fearful stench, similar to that coming from a dead body, which was due not only to the lepers themselves, but also to the food that they use, consisting chiefly of rotten fish. This food is generally eaten by the inhabitants of the Sredni Viluisk Oulousse; it is called chochtu and siema, and is prepared, from small lake fish called mundu, in the following way. Some of these fish are dried in the sun, in a very careless fashion, without any preliminary cleaning; it is then called chochtu, and used for soup; some are put in a specially prepared hole in the ground, which is covered with bark of tree, and, when thoroughly decomposed, is called siema, and used as food, without salt or bread; the latter is not even used by the wealthy Yakuts, whereas the poor people have no idea of it at all.

Some lepers have wives and children, and are able to rear cattle in a very small way. They also hunt hares, squirrels, ermines, and foxes. The skins of these animals, it is said, they use only for themselves, as healthy Yakuts will never venture to take anything from the hands of a leper; but this last statement may be doubted. In 1887 the administration of the Sredni Viluisk Oulousse had the names of fifty lepers; but in reality there must be, if not three times, at least twice as many as those lepers who are not of the poorest class, endeavour in every possible way to remain in their homes, thus hiding the disease from the others. To ascertain the right number of lepers, it would necessitate a strict individual inspection of the whole of the population of the Sredni Viluisk Oulousse.

The disease has passed into the neighbouring oulousse, that is, the Verchni Viluisk Oulousse, where ten men are already noted to have the disease. In the villages of Tchougouisk, Chalbatsk, and Namsk, the disease is not on the decrease, but, on the contrary, on the increase, because, *firstly*, the lepers who live by the lakes—Oupardach of the Louchinsky Nassleg (Yakut village), and Djikimda of the Monkoutchinski Nassleg—wash themselves in the summer in these lakes, as well as throw into them all their refuse, thus contaminating and infecting the water, which is used for food by the healthy natives living on the opposite side; *secondly*, from the numbers of lepers who are still hiding amongst the healthy Yakuts, for fear of being sent into the depth of the forest; *thirdly*, from the very bad hygienic and sanitary conditions of the life of the natives, and on account of the food which we have already described, and which they continually use.

In view of protecting the general health of the people, Mr. Schachourdine, the local ispravnick, made the following propositions to the native administration of Sredni Viluisk on the 14th of March, 1888, under No. 139, and to the starostas of the nasslegs. *First,* to build in three different places, at some distance from the dwellings of the healthy natives, three Russian izbas (Russian peasant-houses), with all the necessary outbuildings, in a locality where there would be running water, and to use them as shelters for the lepers, two of the houses for men, and the third specially for women. *Secondly,* the expense for maintaining these unfortunate sufferers was to be met yearly by the whole oulousse, and not only by those villages from which the lepers came. *Thirdly,* to strictly watch the lepers, so as to prevent the men and women having any communication, and that they should not leave their dwellings under a strict threat of being thrust back into the forest whence they had been taken. Under these conditions, Mr. Schachoudine thought the lepers would not hide themselves, but would come and settle in this shelter, which would be provided with all necessaries, and also, communication between the sexes being prevented, the possibility would be gained of freeing the population altogether of lepers, as they would gradually die out. However, the native chiefs of the said oulousse seemingly were not willing to better the condition of their present dirty existence. On the 20th January of the past year, on receipt of the proposition made by Mr. Schachourdine, they gave a negative answer. At the same time they made the following comment to the proposition under No. 139 :—" We have heard the proposition made by the Viluisk Provincial Ispravnick, No. 135, respecting the organisation of the shelter for the lepers. We will discuss the above proposition and fulfil it when free from the corn and tribute tax, and when the condition of the rural economy of the natives of the Sredni Viluisk Oulousse will be bettered."

In reporting the above, the tchinovnick Schachourdine adds that the organisation of shelters for the lepers and vigilant supervision will check the crimes that take place amongst them. The investigtaion into the said crimes is always accompanied with much danger for the doctors, and other official people, who are bound by their office to question the lepers and to examine leper bodies. At the same time, should the investigation be successfully accomplished, it will hardly ever carry its purpose, as it is not possible to punish lepers convicted of crime by bodily punishment or by sentence of penal servitude.

According to information gathered during the visit of the Governor to the Viluisk Circuit, by personal conversation with the Golova, the Secretary, and the starostas of the six nasslegs of the Sredni Viluisk Oulousse, we see that, from 1887, the disease spread from nine to eleven nasslegs of the said oulousse; that there were cases of leprosy already in the Verchni Viluisk Oulousse, where formerly the disease had not existed; that the number of lepers of the nasslegs had augmented since 1887 by twelve people, from 33 to 45—that is, more than 36 per cent. in two years; and that, at present, according to private information, there are eighty lepers. But this number cannot be considered definite and exact, as many of the lepers try in every possible way to hide their disease, and to remain among their people, so as to escape the miserable fate of their leper brethren.

The doctor had been in 1887, and had visited the lepers living at Hatignach. There were only four lepers at that time; later, the number increased to eight. They live in three yourtas. There is one woman in their number, and a child of ten. The starosta (village elder) saw only one of their number able to walk and chop wood; the other patients were all lying down.

Yankonsky Nassleg, near the River Djerbianga.

Here has lived one leper, alone, for six years; he is a young man. About two versts from his hut live his mother and brother, who bring him his food and place it just inside the door, but never go in, for fear of contagion. The patient is always lying, and it is with great difficulty that he can move or crawl, which he is obliged to do, to light his fire and prepare his food.

The Viluisk police administration has been instructed to gather information about the present number of lepers in the Viluisk Circuit, and, at the same time, to obtain the different names of the places where they are placed, and the distance of each place. The number presented of the lepers in the Viluisk Circuit does not show the exact number of lepers; there are far more, as in these numbers are not included those who are suspected of leprosy, but still remain with their healthy families and relations, as well as the wealthy lepers who are able to hide themselves for some long time without being discovered, until the disease gets to its severe form. From the long existence of leprosy the thinly-populated and poorest Sredni Viluisk Oulousse is over-burdened by its leper members and their poverty-stricken families; that is the reason why the arrears of their Government taxes and social corn taxes are always on the increase.

According to the personal information of the Golova, the secretary of the Sredni Viluisk Oulousse, as well as of the six starostas of the nasslegs, almost all the lepers belong to the poorer natives, so that the maintenance of them, as well as paying the taxes for them, lies as a heavy weight on their separate native communities. Therefore, Government help is considered by the population as absolutely necessary, if it were only in freeing the lepers from the arrears of their taxes. In general, leprosy and its spread is considered by the natives to be their greatest calamity, and they beg for immediate help from the local government.

No less consideration and attention is demanded by the position of the lepers themselves, which is in reality miserable and even dreadful. The duties of Christianity, as well as philanthropy and Government care, do not allow of any further inactivity in this most important business, which appeals at once for resolute measures to be taken for checking this ever-growing national calamity. In view of this the Government directed the Committee to pay special attention to this question, seemingly forgotten for many years, and at once to bring it up for considera- tion; also what measures and what means can be found, and applied, to give help to the lepers, and to better the condition of their lives, and also to prevent the further spread of the disease, and, in fact, to check it altogether.

The Medical Inspector Smirnoff states that leprosy has as yet been but little investigated. The existence of leprosy in the Viluisk Circuit has been known for many years past, and different cases of the disease have been yearly placed in the medical reports. From the docu- ments existing in the inspection and in the provincial administration, we see that the local administration has tried to check the disease; but all their efforts were fruitless, or could not be continued for lack of means.

It is the general opinion that the cause of the disease must exist in the local condition of the country, as well as in the household condition of the Sredni Viluisk Oulousse natives. The country, as is already known, is very thinly populated, and has an abundance of stagnant waters. The household conditions of the native inhabi- tants are most miserable. The filth, the lack of food and water, the use of rotten fish without salt, etc., all this, we may suppose, helps to spread the disease.

At the same time the attention of the Committee was directed to the following:—that, to check leprosy, measures had been taken from 1860 to 1882 by sending special doctors and organising special hospitals, which, however, were closed; and that, in view of the importance of the present state of things, and the lack of full details, it is absolutely necessary to get more thoroughly acquainted with the local condition of the district, and of the disease; also, with all the different conditions of the life of the natives; but, owing to the small number of medical men and the lack of proper scientific appliances in the town of Yakutsk, there is absolutely no one who could undertake this task. The Committee coincided with the above, but stated that, although the present means, both medical and financial, were quite inadequate for the said task, which could only be entrusted to those specially prepared and appointed for it, yet the preparations for further investigation—collecting all details about the spread of leprosy, and about the measures previously taken for it—could be undertaken at present with the means at hand. To accomplish this, it would be necessary to appoint a committee of men, well informed with the local conditions, as well as interested in the said question, who would be able to carry out the above-mentioned work under the direction of the medical inspector, and with the help of the local administration. The accomplishment of this aim, in the sense of deciding the question of the necessary measures and means for checking leprosy—the question being connected with the study of medicine—is anything but an easy one, as it means a good deal of work and expense in investigating the said places. The opinion of the Committee is that it is absolutely necessary to petition the Head Governor of the province for his help in the present work, by sending special people competent for this difficult work of checking the disease, as well as in giving the medical assistance for the investigation of the local conditions, such as the state of the water, of the food, etc.—persons who would be able to bring out how far these conditions aided the spread of leprosy, and who would, at the same time, be able to give good advice about the measures for checking, and altogether exterminating, this disease. The carrying out of all these suggestions, taking into consideration all that has been said above, could only be done when the first steps suggested had been adopted, which will at once clearly show what measures the local administration could take for combating leprosy. It would be desirable to have this information by the month of May of this year, so as to have time to petition the Head Governor of the province for his help in sending competent men during the coming summer, as that is the most convenient time for commencing this work. On this ground the Committee decided as follows:—First, to form a special commission, under the presidency of the Medical Inspector Smirnoff, with the help of the tchinovnick for special services, M. S. Schachourdine, as he had formerly been the Viluisk ispravnick, also the collegiate Councillor Gollmann, as one who had taken part in 1880 in taking measures to prevent the spread of leprosy, and also other people appointed by the president of the commission, who must be well acquainted with the local conditions, and also the position of the disease. The aim of this commission will be to study the documents already existing in the provincial administration concerning leprosy; to make known the former measures which have been taken to check this disease; to explain reasons why these measures have not been carried out or continued; and to gather present information about the condition of the disease, and the best way of combating this disease now, so that when the question may be fully decided by the Provincial Council measures may be adopted in due form.

Secondly, to ask His Excellency if he would not himself give some suggestion in the interest of deciding the present important business.

IX.

MEDICAL INSPECTOR'S REPORT.

To His Excellency, the Civil Governor of the Yakutsk Province.

In presenting the report of my excursion to the villages of Sredni Viluisk, which I undertook by the command of your Excellency, dated January 19th of the present year, No. 175, and of February 14th of the same year, No. 389, I have the honour to report that, according to instruction given, I also visited the nomad villages of Markinsk and Suntar of the Viluisk Circuit, so as to ascertain the needs of the population, with respect to medical assistance. This visit convinced me that the population of the district is totally deprived of the said assistance. The one district doctor, with his two assistant surgeons, is not able to give help to a population of 70,000 souls, scattered over an immense expanse of land, as large as the whole of France, especially as this doctor stationed at Viluisk only leaves the town to visit any part of the district when called by the administration for cases specially demanding legal medical assistance, so that the medical advice he gives to any of the sick natives he finds on his way is only casual, and ends in nothing. The rest of the population, in case of disease, is without any assistance; and yet I have positively ascertained that, among the inhabitants of the district, there are many cases of different diseases, such as ophthalmia, fevers, syphilis, and, from time to time, epidemics of small-pox, chicken-pox, and scarlet fever, whooping cough, and many others.

Syphilis, in its third form, previously studied, is making immense progress, especially in the nomad village of Markinsk, where often cases of the same disease, but in its primary form, may be found. On positive authority it is asserted that syphilis in its primary form is imported from the gold mines, especially from those of Vitim.

Considering the more than pitiable position of the native population of the Viluisk district, my opinion is that it is indispensable to appoint a rural doctor who would have to live in the centre of the district, and to choose several important places in the same district, where assistant surgeons could be appointed, entirely under the direction of the said doctor. My opinion is that it would be best to appoint a feldsher (assistant surgeon) for each nomad village.

(Signed)   MEDICAL INSPECTOR SMIRNOFF.

Information with respect to leprosy gathered during the excursion to the nomad villages of Sredni Viluisk for the purpose of checking the spread of the said disease.

Arriving at Viluisk on February 24th of the present year, I gave notice to the local police to inform all the starostas (chiefs of the village) of the villages of Sredni Viluisk that they had to appear on March 3rd at the local administration of Sredni Viluisk, where they would learn—First, the purport of my excursion, and to enable them personally to give me all information, how many lepers there were, and where they were to be found, and which was the best way to get at them. Secondly, to decide, with other assistants, the best measures for isolating the lepers, and especially for separating the two sexes, appointing distant localities for each, as far as possible one from the other. It became evident at this meeting that the isolation of the lepers had been strictly observed for some long time past.

The natives, dreading the contagion of leprosy, watch each other very carefully, and as soon as they discover the slightest trace of the existence of the germ of the disease, they at once submit the suspected individual to a formal inspection. This inspection is made by several of the older members of the community, who are well acquainted with the symptoms of the disease. They rarely make any mistakes in their decision ; and, having myself verified seventy-four individuals, stated to be lepers, I only found one woman having another malady, and that was syphilis; though there is a great resemblance in the symptoms of this second disease. Among the lepers I found several who had only fallen victims to the disease quite recently, and, therefore, it was difficult to define the disease accurately. With respect to the separation of the sexes, the community is of opinion that this measure is indispensable, as experience has proved that leper parents give birth to children having the germ of the disease, even when only one of the parents was a leper. But the immediate application of this measure presents great difficulties. Firstly, there not being the necessary number of dwellings, and then the construction of the latter could not be effected until the warm weather sets in. Fully aware of the impossibility of constructing dwellings at present, on account of the winter season, I suggested that the village should divide all the lepers amongst them, keeping the sexes apart. My suggestion was unanimously accepted. Continuing my journey, I presently, myself, made this translocation of sexes, and was convinced that the application of this measure was possible even in winter, and that it was only due to the negligence of the starostas that the two sexes were placed or lodged together.

According to the indications given by the authorities of the village and of the local administration, and provided with a list of the lepers and the places of their dwellings, I began my inspection of the villages. During my excursion I inspected seventy-four individuals suffering from leprosy, and who were separated from the rest of the population. I found amongst them—(1) Five men in perfect health, and five children temporarily well (I shall mention these children later); (2) six individuals recently settled, and not mentioned on the list; (3) two individuals suffering from other diseases—one from syphilis and the other from inflammation of the sinews of both hands. This latter patient was only suspected of having leprosy. In general, I found sixty-two adult lepers and five children temporarily well, which makes sixty-seven individuals altogether; (4) thirteen individuals already dead, but not taken off the list; and (5) ten individuals who could not be found. Three of these, according to the reports of the inhabitants, were hiding not far from Gigansk.

The disease, according to the most scientific investigation, manifests itself under two quite different forms— *Lepra Tuberculosis* and *Lepra Anæsthetica.*

The first form is called tuberculosis, because the skin of the face and of the body gradually becomes uneven and rough, and is covered with pimples of different forms and dimensions. In general, this form has a great resemblance to syphilis in its third form, and the same destructive power is observed. In the two cases the cartilages of the roof of the mouth and of the nose and of the larynx are attacked and destroyed, and, at the same time, the extremities of the joints get lacerated, and, very probably, the interior organs as well, such as the liver and lungs. This form of the disease is specially noticed among the inhabitants of the second and third and partly of the fourth, Toguisky village, which is next to the others. Second, the *Anæsthetic* form of leprosy is the most prevalent. This second form of the disease does not inspire as much horror and disgust. The face and body generally remain perfectly pure, and only very rarely are covered with very slight pale eruptions. The eye-brows and the eye-lashes completely disappear. Although the nutriment of the body remains unaltered, what is strikingly observed at the very beginning of the disease is the over-filling of the subcutaneous veins, especially on the chest, so that the skin appears to be covered with a dark-coloured net, and they completely lose the possibility of feeling even the sense of pain. The power of movement remains un-impaired. In cases of this form of the disease, the slow and painless loss of the fingers and toes, as far as the cartilages, is observed. The loss of larger parts of the body I did not notice. The greater part of them died of chronic inflammation of the lungs. As regards the con-tagion of leprosy, the natives state that not only is it hereditary, but certainly contagious, and is communi-cated by the leper to those in perfect health. But to this general rule there are sometimes exceptions, and the same natives showed me several married couples, who, though living together, had not transmitted the disease one to the other.

I found among the lepers five individuals in perfect health. Three of these were very poor, and of their own accord had settled with their parents. The other two had been isolated, as being suspected of having leprosy. The natives told me that up to the present time they have never known a case where healthy individuals, living with lepers of their own accord, had got the disease. However, when I wished to separate five children, aged about ten years, and who appeared in perfect health, the natives positively objected to this, stating that, as the disease was hereditary, and the parents of these children had been lepers, the children would, sooner or later, inevitably become lepers also. The apparent healthy state generally lasts up to the age of fourteen, and, after that, the disease makes its appearance and becomes dangerous for those around. Experience has proved that children who appeared in perfect health have, later on, developed the disease, and communicated it to healthy individuals near them. In reality, I had the occasion to observe several adults, who were born in the colony of leper parents, with marked symptoms of the disease. In the village of Makout-chinsky a little girl of twelve already had the first signs of the disease, such as pains of the arms and legs, loss of the eye-brows, and eye-lashes, dryness of the skin, and a particular inexplicable expression of the eyes, especially characteristic in this disease.

The Conditions of Existence of the Lepers.

The authorities of the district and the inhabitants in general endeavour to settle the lepers in so-called dead places, unfit for the use of the healthy, and, at the same time, as far away as possible from all other habitations, roads, tracks, and footpaths. Huts are built for them in the middle of the forest in dead places, and in the close vicinity of small lakes. These huts are provided with chimneys, but not with any of the indispensable household utensils. It is only the poorest natives that get this terrible disease; the rich, and even those tolerably well-off, seldom have it. Food is provided for these unfortunate people by the community, once or twice a week, and consists of meat, fish, in various forms (more often sour and rotten), tea and milk. The patients did not complain of the insufficiency of food: some even said that, when in health, they were never fed as well.

It sometimes happens that the food is not brought to them at the appointed time, and the patients have to suffer from hunger, for two or three days; but these cases are rare. It is only against the isolation, the want of medical assistance, and the complete inaction, that their complaints are incessant. One is struck at the smallness of the nomad huts they live in; the light hardly penetrates, and the air is so infected by the conglomeration of the patients, the dirt and exhalations from the rotten fish, that one is suffocated on entering them. These unfortunate beings have neither beds nor linen, and their clothing consists solely of sheep-skins and cow-skins all in rags. And it is in these conditions, without any change, that they are obliged to live tens of years, till at last death releases them. Not far from these nomad huts are graves with crosses, showing the spots where the lepers bury each other. Some villages, such as the second, fourth, and partly third Toguisky, are an exception, and show an example to the others, by providing their lepers with larger and better aired huts, building them in less savage localities, thus forming a kind of colony. The locality they have chosen is near a lake, and is not only good but picturesque; the huts are spacious and light. Besides the huts there are other constructions indispensable for a household. The patients are provided with nine cows and fields, and thus lead a life which does not differ in any way from the lives of the natives in general. The one thing that these sufferers need is medical help, which is indispensable, especially as leprosy is often complicated with syphilis. I add lower, the detailed itinerary of my excursion in the colonies, with a short account of the conditions of existence in each one, and the number of patients each one shelters. Besides this, I state the directions I gave about separating the sexes, so as to prevent possible births, and the way this separation had to be carried out. Person-

ally I separated thirteen individuals, with the exception
of some women, too old, or in too advanced a state of
disease, to bear children; these I left where I found
them.

Details of the Excursion to the Nomad Villages of Sredni Viluisk.

The 4th March, 1891, I visited the first group of lepers
in the village called third Toguisky.

The lepers live in a small hut built in a place not far
from the lake Hatignach, and about seven versts distant
from the local administration. The above-mentioned
hut is not sufficient in size for the number of lepers it
shelters. The door is so small that one is obliged to bend
to be able to enter. The hut is very low and hardly any
light enters, and the atmosphere is so foul that even the
fire which is continually burning in the fire-place cannot purify it. The filth of this hovel is disgusting; it
contains a dirty table, and a few benches covered with
filthy skins in lieu of beds, and nothing else. I found
six men and three women huddled together in this
infected hovel. It is inexplicable how so many people
can be lodged in so small and low a hut. The clothes of
these lepers consist of skins (of cows) all in rags and
holes. The form of the disease is anæsthetic. The lepers
do not complain of the lack of food. Besides the nine
lepers that I found, there was a tenth on the list that
died some time past, and had not been scratched off the
list up to now.

As there was no special separate dwelling in the
village of Toguisky, I ordered the Golova (chief of the
tribe) to translocate Marie Egoroff to the village of
Loutchinsk, and to place her in the hut with another
woman, Anna Kirolova, also a leper, living alone with
her son aged two years.

LOUTCHINSK VILLAGE.

I reached this village on the 6th March. It is situated about one hundred versts from the local administration. Twenty versts farther there is a hut which is inhabited by a family consisting of three people; and seventy versts beyond this hut there is another, also inhabited by a family of three persons; twenty-five versts farther still is another hut, in which live one woman and her little son aged two years. On the other side of the local administration, about thirty versts distant, there are two more huts—one inhabited by one man and two women, and the other by one man only, who was brought to where I was stopping, as it was not possible to get to him, even on horseback. The conditions under which these lepers exist were the same as in the village we have just described, only with respect to sanitary arrangements, they were a little better off, as there is not so close a conglomeration of lepers here. In one hut I found three individuals, the woman alone being a leper; her husband and her daughter, aged seventeen, were quite well, and had of their own accord consented to live with the leper mother. There were five individuals on my list, marked dead; but I found a mistake in one case, that of the girl Marie Ivanova. The natives state that, although there is a great distance between the huts, the lepers succeed in visiting each other. I gave an order to the legal authorities to be stricter in watching the lepers, so as to prevent these visits, threatening them that, in case of negligence respecting these orders, they would be responsible to the local administration, and would be obliged to educate the children that might ensue from these visits.

The Village of Tebinsk.

The first group of lepers in this village consisted of four people, and were placed at a distance of thirty versts from the small village Olbout. I visited this hut the 10th March. At a distance of 100 versts from the first group lived two lepers, husband and wife, and to reach them one is obliged to pass the two villages of Kobiansk and Kakouisk. Besides that, a little aside from Tebinsk, there is a leper living isolated and alone. The conditions under which these lepers of the village of Tebinsk exist are the same as in the two preceding ones.

The Village Kakouisk.

The hut inhabited by the lepers is placed at the distance of ninety versts from the first group of lepers of the village of Tebinsk. I visited them the 12th March. This hut is inhabited by two lepers. The conditions of existence are always the same.

The Village of Kobiansk.

The hut in which four lepers are placed is too small for them, and the chimney is all in ruins, and ought to be renovated. Among these four lepers is a woman who is not a leper at all. She came with a sister, who was a leper, and, after this sister died, was not allowed to return, but was compelled to remain with the lepers.

The Village of Mukutchinsk.

To reach this village, situated at a distance of twenty-five versts from the administration, we had to turn back on our way and pass through the villages of Tebinsk and Loutchinsk.

I got there on the 15th March. About twenty versts distant from the local administration, and a little aside in the forest, is a hut inhabited by ten lepers. One can imagine under what condition they live. Among them, four individuals are in perfect health. Nicholas Vasilieff was placed with the lepers because his parents had been lepers. Ivan Michailoff has been accustomed from his childhood to live with lepers, and remains with them of his own accord. Pelagie Zacharova accompanied her husband of her own accord, who died. As I insisted that these four individuals, who were healthy, should be allowed to return, the natives answered that they would not object to it, but that they knew that these individuals would be obliged to return to the lepers, as no one would allow them to settle near them for fear of contagion. Two little girls were born in this place, one of them already showing signs of this disease. I at once ordered that the women should be separated, especially Pelagic Zacharova; but the order could not be carried out at once, as there was no empty hut for them. The community promised to build a hut about forty versts away from the last-mentioned one, and to place the women there. In this way there will be two sections in the village; one for men, and one for women. The starosta (head of the village) is obliged to see this order carried out, and to apprise the local administration as soon as the hut is built.

About 200 versts from this colony is another one built not far from the lake Mastach. I have already mentioned that four villages—the second, third, fourth Toguisky, and partly Kirguidaiski—have organised a sort of colony for their lepers. This colony is composed of large and clean huts, and even other buildings indispensable for household management. Besides that the lepers have fields for their cattle. which is also provided for them Meat, fish, tea, and other provisions are sent them every week. Thanks to these measures the lepers live comfortably, but, unfortunately, the form of their disease is of a very bad nature, and quickly destroys the whole organism, giving the lepers a most awful appearance. This form is observed only in the last-named colony. It is the tuberculosis form, and has a syphilitic basis. In verifying the list of lepers, I found that in the third Toguisky village there are ten lepers, three of whom were absent; in the second Toguisky, four lepers, one absent; in the fourth Toguisky, ten lepers; and at last in the village of Kirguidaiski only one leper. I gave instructions to remove five women, and as there was a hut about eighty versts distant, which had formerly been occupied by lepers but now empty, the community promised at once to translocate these five women, and to apprise the local administration of that fact. In the Kirginsk village three lepers were mentioned, but I found none. In the village of Genkoust I found three Tongus, two of them lepers, and the third suffering from another disease. In the village of Namsk, two lepers.

(Signed) SMIRNOFF,
Medical Inspector.

X.

Résumé of some of the difficulties of my journey among the lepers. Being a translation of a document written by myself in French, and signed by the tchinovnick who acted as my interpreter.

We left Yakutsk for Viluisk June 22nd, 1891, to begin our long journey of three thousand versts (2000 miles) on horseback, for the purpose of visiting the lepers living in forests unknown, even to the Russians. Our cavalcade

was somewhat curious, consisting of about fifteen men and
thirty horses; all those around me were talking in a
language which I could not understand, though Mr. Petroff
did, who also knew a little French. The photographer
in Yakutsk took our photograph; but someone moved
before it was finished, and therefore it was a failure. It
might have given an idea of our costumes. As to mine,
it was not very elegant: a sun-hat, over it a network
arrangement as a protection from the mosquitoes, a jacket
with very long sleeves, with the badge of the red cross
on my left arm. Very full trousers down to my knees,
and high boots above my knees. A revolver, a whip, and
a little travelling bag. I was obliged to ride as a man
for many reasons. First, because the Yakutsk horses
were so wild that it was impossible for me to ride otherwise; second, no woman could ride on a lady's saddle for
3000 versts; and thirdly, as there were no roads, the
horse constantly stumbles on the roots that are in the
forest, threatening to throw the rider over its head; then
it sinks into the mud till the rider's feet are on earth;
having somehow recovered its footing, it rushes along
between the branches of the trees and shrubs, utterly
regardless of the fact that they were tearing and making
mincemeat of the rider's dress. The first day we did five
versts ($3\frac{1}{3}$ miles); the second, fifteen (10); the third,
twenty ($13\frac{1}{3}$); and after that, 80 versts without stopping
for sleep. One's sufferings were far worse than even
when travelling in the tarantass; the stiffened position
of my body being altogether contrary to its usual free and
easy habit; and the jerky movements of the untrained
horse gave me dreadful pain.

We were obliged to take food with us for three months;
some black and white dried bread, some dried prunes,
some tea and sugar, and other indispensable articles for so
long a journey; for, excepting at Viluisk, you can get
absolutely nothing, not even bread and tea.

Before leaving Yakutsk, His Grace the Archbishop asked us to go to his house, that he might give us his blessing. When we went, His Grace, dressed in all his most brilliant robes, blessed us and pronounced over us his benediction. All the time I was in Yakutsk he took care of me like a father, tenderly and lovingly. We left there very quietly, so as not to attract attention. I had a very great objection to make any parade of our starting to my work, for it was serious; and it is my desire that it should be finished as it was begun, with the blessing of God on us at every step, whether that step be difficult or easy.

When you are travelling through marshes in which your horse, without a moment's warning, sinks up to his stomach, you are obliged to hold on by the reins and by your knees and hands and every way, as best you can. The only thought in my mind at the time was to keep on and not fall off, and to keep my horse on his feet, for if my horse fell I must fall with it, and find myself in the mud. The first ten marshes it was not so difficult; but after we had passed hundreds of them all the body ached; I felt as though I had spent fifty years on the tread-mill· It was then, that, to keep in the saddle, was a feat worthy of a hero.

On the official maps there is a road traced leading from Yakutsk to Viluisk, but in reality there is no such road— so do not be misled by official maps if you should go there. You will have to pass through unnamed marshes, and never find any such road.

During the summer the mosquitoes are frightful, both in the night and in the day; and when you arrive at a yourta, which serves as a post-station, the dirt and vermin and smell are simply disgusting; bugs, lice, fleas, etc., cover the walls, as well as the benches on which you have to sleep. Even on the ground you will find them, and, as soon as a stranger comes in, it seems as if the insects make a combined assault on him in large battalions; and, of course, sleep is a thing never dreamed of. After a few days the body swells from their bites into a form that can neither be imagined nor described. They attack your eyes and your face, so that you would hardly be recognised by your dearest friend. Yet with all these pains and penalties we had still to continue riding from forty to eighty versts in one day; we did even 100 versts without sleep. The fatigue, and the want of rest were dreadful. Cows and calves were in the same yourta with us, and the smell from them and from everything else was horrible. We would, indeed, have made very funny pictures of miserable travellers. As there is only one yourta at a post-station, ladies and gentlemen are obliged to sleep all together, and any traveller that may be present at the same time; a gentleman might put up with it, but it is impossible for a lady. After riding on horseback for the first time, my body was in constant pain, and complete rest with the possibility of undressing was indispensable; but as they say in French, "*à la guerre comme à la guerre.*" As undressing was not possible, I was obliged to rest the best way I could. The Cossack was also ill that day, and Mr. Petroff and myself had our heads bound up so as to ease the pain a little, having been badly burnt by the sun. To have even five minutes' rest we were obliged to have a fire made up of cowdung in this disgusting yourta, and, to prevent the smoke from escaping, as that is the only way to have any rest, we were obliged to cover the opening of the chimney. The mosquitoes left us alone; but as to our eyes, they were so irritated by the smoke that they were bathed in tears; and my head suffered even worse. The other animals, however, did not cease to attack us all the time. I would indeed have presented an original picture. To remain five minutes longer within was not possible, we could do nothing at all because of the smoke; and this continued all day.

Really, I think the sufferings of this journey have added twenty years to my age. But I would willingly do it ten times over to aid my poor lepers who are placed in the depths of these unknown forests.

You are always running the risk of being attacked by bears here, so that we always kept our revolvers ready at our side or under our heads; and two Yakuts as sentinels, with large fires at each end of the little encampment.

Soon after we started on our journey, we were obliged to travel in the night, because our horses had no rest in the day time from the terrible horse-flies that were quite dangerous there. They instantly attacked the wretched beasts, so that it was an awful sight to see our horses with the blood running down their sides, many of them becoming so exhausted that they were not able to carry our luggage.

At one place the bears might have attacked us with impunity. It was a very dangerous spot, as we were in the depths of a thick forest; we could hardly see two yards off, and the Yakuts saw eleven bears as we passed. Before starting, we all grasped our revolvers and guns, and we always had a large box filled with stones, which made a great clatter as we travelled; the bells also of some of our horses made a considerable noise. One of the Cossacks was in front of me, Mr. Petroff was on one side, the other Cossack and the rest of the escort, the horses and luggage, being behind. In the less dangerous parts of the forest everyone used to sing, making noise enough to frighten fifty bears. The horses are in such a fearful dread of the bears that they smell them afar off; and, as soon as they know they are near, they become almost unmanageable, dragging you through the forests, between the trees, flying like the wind. One thing was perfectly clear, that had the bears come near, it is quite certain some of us would have been killed, if not by the bears, then by the horses, who were almost mad.

One further danger must be related, so that readers of this document may have some notion of the many trials that had to be endured. After having left Viluisk one night we entered an immense forest, where the horses made a peculiar noise with their feet, as if they were walking over hollow ground. Having asked what it meant, I was told that we were near a place where the forest was burning. In about half an hour there was seen in the distance a small body of flames; but on getting nearer it seemed almost a picture of the infernal regions, so terrible was it to the sight, and yet we were obliged to go right into it. Far as could be seen there were flames and smoke rising from the ground, which was everywhere, apparently, burning. One of the Yakuts was in front; I was next, my horse picking its way; but sometimes it would get into a hole where there was fire, when it became terrified, throwing itself from right to left, becoming restive and wild till one became almost exhausted; for, in addition to this, there was the effort to distinguish the path through the smoke with eyes smarting and almost blinded with the glare of the fire. However, we travelled on, but all at once we heard a dreadful noise behind us. Nothing could be seen through the flames and smoke, but the noise steadily kept coming nearer; our horses began to get still more restless, and before we could have any idea where the sound came from, a horse with some luggage on it, mad with fright at the flames and the smoke, rushed into our midst. Mr. Petroff, who was behind, had just time to give it a slash with his whip, which made it turn a little to the right, otherwise it would have been on me, and certainly I would have been killed. It was quite mad, and dashed right into the flames, as it was impossible to stop it, having so much to do to manage our own horses.

This was the most terrible experience of the journey, and it was only through God's mercy that we were kept alive.

I have asked Mr. Petroff to sign this, as he was witness to these dangers, having been with me all the time.

(Signed)   KATE MARSDEN.

August 24th (September 6th), 1891.

(Signed)   SERGE MICHAILOVITCH PETROFF,
            Tchinovnick for special services attached
                to the Governor of Yakutsk.

XI.

*Résumé of my journey into the Viluisk Province, Siberia, being
the translation of a document written by myself in French
and signed by the tchinovnick, who acted as my interpreter.*

In Viluisk I consulted with several persons as to the condition of the lepers in that province, and I was assured that it was dreadful, that they were thrust out by the community into immense forests, without any-thing with which to cover themselves; and the yourtas, or huts, in which they live are so small that they were packed in them more like animals than human beings. We were said to have gone 2500 versts (1666 miles) on horseback; but as the Yakuts have no idea of the length of a verst, I am sure we must have gone over 3000; for frequently, when we were told that there were only ten versts to such and such a place, we found there were twenty.

The community, having heard that I had come to help them (non-officially), were so grateful and happy that they cleared a road in the forest for 1500 versts, where, otherwise, it would have been impossible to pass. They also built small bridges over the most dangerous marshes; but to accomplish this, they had to put aside all their agricultural work for the summer, which was certainly a loss to them. It was all the more gratifying to hear that they did it of their own free will. Everywhere along the road they showed me every possible kindness, begging me most earnestly to help their lepers.

A great difficulty I experienced was that I did not understand either the Russian or Yakutsk language, and being accompanied only by about thirty men, all of whom spoke in a language unknown to me. It was indeed most awkward for a lady to be alone under such circumstances in a foreign country. Mr. Petroff spoke a little French, so it was only through him that I could make myself understood.

The 3rd (15th) July, 1891, the ispravnick, the doctor (feldsher), two soldiers, Mr. Petroff and myself, left Viluisk for the leper dwellings in the Mastach district, near the lake Abungda, where the largest colony of them is situated.

We descended the river Viluie for about twenty versts, where we were met by the chief of the starostas and the Yakuts, about twenty men, with thirty horses; all were waiting to conduct us to the place to which we were going.

After we had some tea we entered the forests, and having gone up the hill for about twenty versts we stopped on seeing a fire, which is always a sign of some-one being near, and inquired how far we had still to go before we could find drinkable water, and grass for our horses. As Mr. Petroff was talking, I noticed something moving between the trees of the forest. I asked what it was, and was told that it was a leper-child who wanted to ask me to help him. I dismounted and went towards him; but the poor child, thinking that I would be frightened at his disease, as the Yakuts are, kept going backwards, and it was difficult to make him understand that I wanted to speak with him, and even touch him. I then spoke to his mother and brother, who told me the history of this poor child.

The community, having affirmed that he was a leper (and it must be understood that in this community there was not a single Russian, nor any man that had any idea of medicine), ordered this child to live alone in the forests in a yourta, that had been built for him about ten versts away from his mother, and, further, that he was to remain there for the rest of his life. Thank God, his mother took pity on him in his solitude, and built a tiny shed behind her yourta, where the child used to come secretly, as soon as it was dark, to sleep. But had the society found this out, the mother would have been punished by also being thrust into the depths of the forest and separated from the rest of the community.

This touching story proved the truth of all the cruelties that I had been told were practised on the poor lepers. We gave him every possible help, and the ispravnick took the child under his protection, which will prevent a repetition of such cruelties.

As for the consequences of this journey for all of us, but especially for me—a lady alone, who up to that time had never ridden on horseback, and was now obliged to ride like a man, the Yakut horse being unmanageable otherwise (indeed, along this dreadful road there was no possibility of riding otherwise)—the many difficulties, the fatigue, and want of proper and clean food, the danger from the bears that abound in the Viluisk province, the dangers of travelling in the night through dark forests, the roots of the trees interlacing the roads so that the horse is constantly stumbling against them, the cold at night, and the heat during the day, the strain on your eyes in trying to peer through the darkness, the dampness, the absence of any

habitation near, and often only disgusting water to drink—
all this will perhaps give you a little idea of some of our
sufferings.

But I will not speak much about them, as the object of
my task is not to tell what we endured, but to bear witness to the sufferings of the wretched lepers, and, with
God's blessing, to put into this work all my strength, all
my heart, and all my life ; and I pray in the name of the
Lord that every Christian will help them by his prayers,
and his money, in their terrible condition.

About sixty versts (forty miles) from Abungda the
priest of the district met us. We rested at his house, and
then he conducted us to Abungda. As we neared the
dwellings of the lepers, the road got more difficult and
impassable, for the lepers are always located in the
farthest and loneliest places, those least frequented, and
the most difficult of access, in order to prevent them
returning to their former homes. We travelled along the
lake, and as we came out of the forest we saw the yourtas
where the lepers live.

They were expecting us, and as soon as they saw us we
were saluted. After giving them every help and assistance we could, we all prayed together; and Her Majesty
the Empress was not forgotten. I know that these
prayers will be heard. It was terribly sad to listen to
the feeble voices of these weak lepers ; to see them on
their knees making the sign of the Cross with their poor
maimed hands, often without fingers and without strength,
so that they could hardly lift up their arms ; their faces
frightfully disfigured by this disease ; in their eyes you
could read that all hope was lost. Their feet were toeless,
so that some could not walk at all, and could only drag
along their bodies with the help of a low stool. This
picture of a dying life, without any consolation, touched
us so deeply that the remembrance of it will remain
with us all our days. In this place there were two

yourtas about thirty yards apart; and between them
seven graves, as if to take away the possibility of these
poor creatures forgetting for one moment that death
always follows them, and is always near.

When a leper dies he remains in the same yourta, with
the living, for three days. Will you just look into the
interior of this yourta? It is so small that the inmates
are obliged to sleep on the benches along the wall, without any mattress, and so near to each other that the feet
of one leper touch the head of the next, whilst the others
have to sleep on the bare earth, these yourtas having no
floors. There is a frightful odour from this disease, and
the cold in the winter is so terrible that when the door is
opened for a minute one is almost frozen. The cows are
in the same hut, and the dead bodies have to remain there
on the benches, adding to the frightful stench of the
lepers. When the coffin is brought a leper is obliged to
go out in the terrible cold, and drag as best he can the
coffin into the hut, put the corpse into it, and, after that,
put it on an old sledge and drag it for some yards to the
grave. Indeed, these people have been cruelly forsaken
and forgotten; but it is hoped that a brighter time is
about to dawn for them, and that the greatest bitterness
of their sorrow will soon be of the past.

When they had the small-pox there no one visited
them, neither the doctors nor any of the Yakuts; they
were obliged to bear the sufferings of this disease also
quite alone, without any one to aid them; no beds for
their suffering bodies, and almost without clothes, with
the exception of the disgusting shoubas (fur cloaks), which
only augmented the irritation so terrible in this disease.
What they endured no one will ever know.

There was a girl of eighteen in this yourta, who had
lived all her life with the lepers, though she was in
perfect health. Her mother had been a leper, therefore
the community ordered her to remain always with them.

After consulting with the ispravnick, the priest, the doctor, and Mr. Petroff, we decided not to leave the place until this girl was freed. The kind ispravnick said that when she was washed and dressed in other clothes, he would willingly take her into his own house; and before we left Viluisk we saw the girl settled with him.

At Abungda the lepers had cows; and certainly this was the best place we visited, although even here the yourta in which they lived was only six yards long and four yards broad; and there were eleven lepers in it. Such conditions are quite unsuitable for these poor creatures, as they have to spend eight or nine months of the year in this place, or in another just as bad. All the other leper settlements we visited were worse and worse.

At one place, Djikinda, there was a man, a woman, and two children almost naked. In another place, Ilgidjan, there were six people almost naked. The men, women, and children live all together more like animals than human beings.

In another place, Abalack Kel, I saw a woman who had been condemned by the community to live all alone for the rest of her life; she had already been isolated for four years. She saw no one but her husband regularly, who brought her food and firing. She very rarely saw her children—then only at a long distance, as they never dared go near her. Thus, in this perfect, endless solitude, she has to live always. Her work in winter was to drag her body along the snow the best way she could, as she was not able to walk, to fetch the food that was taken to her by her husband, and left at some yards away from the hovel. If she had any strength she kindled a fire; if not, she had to remain in the cold.

Again, at another place, Harialach-Kell, there were three men who lived alone. They told me that the bears often frightened them by coming close to the yourta; but, luckily, they had a very clever dog, who used to bark incessantly at them till he chased them back into the forest, often returning without any voice left. Had it not been for this dog the bears would have entered the yourta, as the poor lepers have neither guns nor revolvers.

At a place named Honkeil, there was a man who had come a long distance to ask for my help; he said that the bears were his only companions, and that he had also a dog to protect him; he was likewise condemned to live alone in the forest.

Neither man, woman, nor child are exempt from this cruelty. Once the community decides that anyone is a leper he is thus condemned; even if he himself is not a leper, but if his parents have been lepers, or he has lived with lepers, it is the same; for life he is condemned to isolation.

In some places the yourtas are small, even for two people; but we found as many as eight and ten people in them. The dirt, the frightful odour from the lepers, the absence of any sanitary place, their food, chiefly consisting of fish, and often rotten fish, butter and grease that they drink, and bark of trees, and their disgusting clothes, will hardly give you an idea of the miserable conditions under which they barely exist. It is true what Father John of Viluisk says, that in all the world you will not find people in a more lost condition than they are. The terror the Yakuts have of this disease is remarkable; nothing in the world would make them touch or go near them. Be it father, mother, or child, they are torn away from their family, and condemned to live alone to the end of their life.

I will give you another instance of the cruelties practised in the name of disease. About twenty versts from Viluisk at the other side of the river Viluie, there was an orphan child, who had an inheritance of some four cows. His parents were dead, and his uncle had charge of him, who, wishing to take possession of these cows, informed the community that his nephew was a leper.

They told him that he was to be isolated like the rest, and they ordered the uncle to have charge of him. The uncle built him a tiny shed—the doctor who saw it said it was not large enough for a dog; the uncle then took the child into the forest where the shed was, and he left him there without providing any food or drink. After some time the child was found dead; he had died from starvation and cold. His uncle had buried him without a coffin, and when the doctor opened his body, he found nothing but a little clay in his stomach. What this poor child must have suffered from terror, hunger, thirst, and cold, no one will ever know. To prevent the possibility of a repetition of a similar case I asked the advice of the Committee, as well as their help, and that of many others.

In another place there was a woman-leper, who used to go near the dwellings of the healthy Yakuts for stealing purposes; the starosta ordered that all her clothes were to be taken away from her so as to prevent her leaving her yourta. However, one day she ventured out without clothes, and her body was found frozen and dead.

We visited the lepers in thirteen different places: but at last I was too ill to go any farther, and neither the ispravnick, Mr. Petroff, nor the doctor, would take the responsibility of letting me go on; so I was obliged to remain in the tent.

At Sredni Viluisk a man was suspected of having leprosy; but as at last it was proved that he really had the disease, they ordered him to be sent thirty versts away, where there were other lepers belonging to the same community. He had neither fingers nor toes, and was so terribly disfigured that I asked them how he was going to be sent. I was answered, "Oh, very well, quite easily." But knowing full well that they consider that the worst things are quite good enough for the lepers, I wanted to be certain as to the manner in which he would be conveyed there. It was only after a great deal of trouble that I could get to the truth; first, I was told that he could walk; but I said, "No, that is impossible;" then they said, "We will put him on a bull." I again said, "No, that is also impossible." Then they said, "On a horse;" but to this I objected; and, at last, after a great deal of discussion, they consented to put him on a sledge, with some hay to lie upon.

Now, I do not think that they even thought that their first propositions were cruel, the Yakuts being so accustomed to walk and ride themselves; but we can well understand that the sufferings of this leper were indeed terrible—the poor man being so ill and so disfigured, needing the best care possible—and the Yakuts wanted to add to his sufferings, as he could not have held himself on a horse. And now, having seen all these things on the spot, I want every one to consider in what way we can ameliorate their condition.

Having witnessed all these horrors, I am going straight to Irkutsk to collect money, with the help of the Committee and others, for a hospital. After that I hope to have the honour of presenting myself to Her Majesty the Empress at Gatchina, and to lay at her feet all these details, with the list of names of those persons who have given money for the hospitals; and I am more than sure that Her Majesty, who is so gracious and tender-hearted, will take all the sufferings of the sick and of the poor to heart, and sustain me in this work. As for myself, I will put all my strength, my health, my life into it, so that the existence of these wretched lepers may be bettered, and that they may have a hospital. But the result of this rests absolutely with the Lord; and it is in His name that I beg Christians everywhere to help them.

This *résumé* of my journey among the lepers I have

asked Mr. Petroff to read, and afterwards to sign, as witness and translator, having accompanied me all through this part of the journey.

KATE MARSDEN.

August 19th (August 31st), 1891.

(Signed)   SERGE MICHAILOVITCH PETROFF,
Tchinovnick for special service to the
Yakutsk Governor.